Infini Entendre

A book of poems

Whickwithy

Infini Entendre

All rights reserved

Copyright © 2012 Whickwithy

ISBN: 978-0-9971412-8-3

This book may not be reproduced in whole or in part in any form without written permission.

Also available in ebook on Amazon.

In honour of the flawless beauty of Life. May this, at least, reflect a glimmer of it.

Poems............1
Index............140

Whickwithy

Poems

The Rainbow Knight

The Rainbow Knight, along the river, walked in prism dreams
The sun was shining on the ripples in chromatic streams
And, now, he pondered light and hue
Once more, the spectral sight in view
Of passion's willing ways
His stride was broken by a thought of life in toneless tale
At the thought, a pain was wrought, that heart and will would fail
The wind picked up and tossed the whim
The river washed it past the rim
To shores of pallid days
He felt, within his glowing heart, the end of burden's blight
The mystic gleam cast, from afar, kaleidoscopic light
And, with the rippled light between
A brilliance settled with a sheen
To set the world ablaze

Small breakthroughs

It's funny how the smallest things in life reflect the large
And, how the microcosm shows the infinite in charge
A slight nuance, a subtle thing, is noticed as a change
It tumbles through the heart and soul, all life to rearrange
Inertia, foolish habits, come steamrolling through the day
But, just a nudge, the slightest push, consumes your every way
To move a mountain's easier than move the drone of life
To break apart mundaneness, live each moment well and rife
No foolishness, no coy belongs, no lack of will or sight
To move momentous mountain, you must push away the fright

The hounds of life

Upon a dismal day
I trudge along
The hounds begin to bay
A haunting song
The pad of life's clawed feet
Race at my back
The fangs that snap for meat
That they do lack
I turn and face the face
Of life's false hope
With passion and a trace
Of life's true scope
A heartbeat's heard alone
Within my ear
That heart of purest tone
Removes all fear
It pumps my blood through all
the time and tear
It wills away the mist
So I can see
The hounds are but the gist
Of what would be
If love were but a whist
In mind, for me

Caverns of the mind

Each poem, like a key, unlocks a cavern in my mind
Vast spaces are encountered with the treasures there to find
All journey's long, the patience laid, transcendence in its deed
The echoes of the cavern's walls reflect a certain creed
Lost inside of canyons, on occasion, I have come
Searching for the reasons in a simple rule of thumb
That all sum up to answers etched so deeply in the wind
There is a life's reality in which tumults rescind
Exploring canyon's resonance has brought the echoes round
There is a way on through without the wind and fury's sound

Whickwithy

The Traveler's tale

Towards the mountains' rugged peaks, I passed through ache and toil
At the very peak of mount, I felt a mystic foil
No intent to let me pass, repelled my will to roam
But, then, a pause, a sudden feel, a friend whose welcomed home
I wandered, then, throughout this land, this land I'll never leave
The path one takes, extend your hand, and never disbelieve
The way was set so long ago, the only need, depart
There is a kernel all good tales deliver to the heart
The steps to take to gain the land on heart and soul are marked
They're scored upon the ways of life, let go and you've embarked
The path is such we all can feel, so deep within's the spark
Conscious thought distorts the path, the rhythm of the hark
This tale is told of brighter things than those of daily dread
The passion of the soul is as the leaven for the bread

Of kings and castles

Of kings and castles long live lores
Like echoes down the corridors
Of castle walls all made of stone
Of kings remains all made of bone
Beyond the dust and crumbled walls
Reverberating, empty halls
The tales are told to split the age
And captivate the stoic sage
The heart that thrums the cord of light
Begets a rainbow to ignite
The king of stone to sudden tear
And castle walls to persevere
Of kings and castles made of stone
On windswept plain, set all alone

Bifrons

One face has faced infinity and revels in the ride
All ruts encountered on the way are taken slow, in stride
Another face of withered stare is on the other side
A burning deep impatience with no thought of fear or pride
The cry of reason stifles as the aching heart does smother
The winds of fate are weathered by the iron of the other
To pass through time, a ghost, the merest wisps of life and sense
While darkly lit, a whisper's heard, the mists, at once, condense
The faces fold, appear as one, the burden set aside
The ache is gone, the heart is one, the tears have all been cried

Passion's play

The flame upon the cheek shoots high and glows so blinding bright
The spiral of the eyes entrance, dilating to delight
The dance upon the lawn is awe
The sigh blinks breath, the line of jaw
The heart upon a kite
The soaring with a flutter
The feelings are all right
The wind picks up to brush along the neck and, then, the cheek
Or, is it kiss, that flushes all, and bends the knees so weak
The whisper seeks to flame the heart
The flame of kiss the dance did start
The head spins on a might
And, now, begins to stutter
But, from eye to eye, it's right
And, now the dance is ending, yet again, it's just begun
The swirling on the lawn of life is just how it is run
The heart will sing as soul meets day
And on we go with Passion's play
All life behold the single sight
Set sail in windswept cutter
As all life is set to right

Realms of the mind

I so often wander there for passion or from plight
I find there always something that will make it feel alright
To fly with face of peacefulness when all is wrought or broken
There is no better place to know the whisper that's not spoken
Vistas of imagining like whispered rivers near
Worlds beyond all patterning, await the silent tear
And, if the cold's beneath the bone
Or whither on, the flight unknown
When spring pulls back to winter's raging
Or, love of life seem surely aging
The peace is in the mind, the hearth is there to call
Always you will find, the heart not aged at all

A fairy tale

The mind, it slowly shatters
As the dawn blows thoughts my way
I sweep up all that scatters
Like the jacks from someone's play
Those lives and all the epic tales, patina on my heart
Stars and moons and all else pales, replaying their own part
Are all those lives, a fairy tale to keep my soul afloat
It's just a guess, 'twill never fail, as song surpasses note
But, one thing that is surely true
I'm wrapped around with love of you
All lives, from start to blessed end
The will for that will always mend
And will's foray will never bend
Our heart and soul, the final blend

More realms of the mind

Realms of mind, I'd wander there
Evermore, no slightest care
But, life calls back the body and cannot be ignored
And, harking back, the mind still calls and always sparkles more
Shoot the ray to spill the beam
Cross to wildness at the stream
Step so high that worlds go past
Yonder reigns new worlds, at last
Flash while striking past the bend
Colored lips will kiss to send
On the way to swirl and foam
Ripple through the sound to roam
Find a wrinkle in the spark
Life will sprinkle bright the arc
Laughter spills along the way
Washing off this wearied stay
Rainbow circles paint the ears
Life unfolds, no time for fears
On and on, beyond the realm
Scattered back to fill the helm
Echo caverns of the mind
There you'll hear and often find
The sighing wind and shifting sands
So deep beneath the hidden lands

Dream vision

I sweep outward a transcending hand and watch the ripples form
They touch upon my darling's land and wash away the storm
As ripples carry on the song, they sing a heightened note
As if concurring with the thought and with the words I wrote
The words that walked away with care and passed thru time's own door
The thought that lingered on the porch as if he knew the score

.

Whickwithy

The weaver and the wizard

The artisan begins his tireless toil
The consequence of all the threads uncoil
The whisper of the weaver's patience tasked
Each thread, an answer to a question asked
But, for the tapestry to answer all
The blend of threaded questions must enthrall
Suspended gaze must answer to the call
The witness of the wizard wherewithal
A tableau that can cast the curing spell
Eliminates inertias that propel
The tapestry unbinds the vile unreason
Transforming life from winter's brutal season
The weaver builds the tapestry from thread
The wizard brings the life to those undead
In colors bright, the tapestry portrays
That life can be more than the pending days
Warm and rich, this life beneath the sun
The weaver and the wizard are as one

Worlds apart

I stand immense with galaxies beneath
The mists condense, the whisper in a sheath
The cosmos spins, all time and space subsume
And coalesce to worlds that burst abloom
Kaleidoscope of wonders through the end
Will and passion, portions of the blend
While worlds apart brings measures quite extreme
Momentous tale we intricately scheme

Lagniappe

Time tells tales to fool us all
Of sky's abyss and morning call
Shocked and shattered by the tale
No more roaring, lesser hale
Look around the last outcrop
Find, indeed, life's sweet lagniappe
Once is not enough for me
In this life, Lagniappe will be
Shout and barrel down the road
Change the tires, change the mode
Slam the door, prepare to pass
Life's the wheels, Lagniappe's the gas
Lagniappe seems to come in vain
Ricochet off the watchman's bane
Pound the fist upon the pavement
Knowing where and what the rave meant
Raging seas and falling toast
Still the one that meant the most
Settle now into the rocket
Metronome in my back pocket
Metro-dome to hold the floods
Lives and nests and narrowed bloods
Bubbling up from pale to first
Knowing now is none the worst
Tickled to the tallest flight
Know it well, Lagniappe's own right
Time tells tales and some are true
Lagniappe for so very few

Whickwithy

The crime

Ah, for me, it is a crime
To go too long without a rhyme
It soothes my soul and lets release
Pent up feelings, cooling feast
It makes such sense of all I am
In many ways, 'tis like a jam
To spread on toast of life I live
To sweeten all, with this I give
To translate from the living frame
To bring it home is why I came
All life is here to celebrate
The rhyme just builds a true portrait
To pass along the love of life
With certainty our hearts are rife
The love for all that lives and breathes
The squirrel, the bird, the brook, the leaves
For beauty's here in all known climes
Heart bursts away in ringing rhymes
Do you feel the joy in this?
The love, the song, the endless bliss
Truly do I sing the praise
Of love and life, I stand amazed
The passions of it all reveal
Hidden not, all life surreal
In wonderment and feelings spent
Across the span of time we're lent
Tumble to the wild wind rocking
Christened to the cusp that's knocking
Poetry is beauty rich
Pressed into the smallest niche

Poetry too

Compress it down, so much to be
No room for waste, so set it free
Leave room for beauty, love and heart
And build the story from the start
With heart and rhyme, my poetry
So often keyed with imagery
At least the favorites that I write
I hate it when there's driveled spite
Arrrrgggghhhhh! A pirate's shout I say!!!
Let's stick to fun and love and play!!!!!!!!!!
Exceptions, they should never rule
The double entendre, favorite tool
Crazy as the night, but glorious to me
My launch is there for ken through wondrous poetry
It comes, to me, like trill of bird
As clear as day, who ever heard?!!?!
My biggest struggle, oft, you see
To stop the flow of words to be..........
!!!!CUT IT OUT!!!!

The gloom

Funereal twins called, once again
Despair and gloom, to take me for a spin
What a ride, it lasted but a flash
I dove to safety just before the crash
I dusted off, a pale and desperate drone
And, wandered back to sanity alone
They wander, cackling, in the depths of night
I smile at them and feign it's recondite

Past Participle

Masked inside the meaning and whither to its way
Spoken with the force of gales, it beckons on to say
What then, you shout, to leave it out
Wherefore, you flout a rocky spout
It flickers on, no more to go
Spoken like a broken blow
The power tickles to the flight
Pass along the sparkling night
The perfect participle has such meaning in its way
Not wasted on the maundering, nor wandering to stray
And spoken like true speakers speak
Not lent on loan, nor shadows bleak
I shuffle on and all the while
Behind those eyes, a hidden smile

Resolve

My resolution coincides
In rampant will it now resides
There is no place beneath the stars
No wind to bend the deodars
I hold on steady to the course
That heart does utterly endorse
The mountaintop with snowy build
Continues on, a cup unfilled
An avalanche, at last, is waged
The crucible was finely gauged
Resolving all, the steel refined
I clasp the hilt, the runes are lined
To tell the tale of loss and gain
And, then, rescind the deepest pain
Tomorrow will be soon enough
The will un-trampled in the rough

Poetry

And, still, what I don't understand
Is poetry's impelling hand
What is this urge to bare the soul
What is this surge that makes me whole
Sometimes the meaning's hidden well
It flashes high to cast its spell
So oft the meaning's clear as glass
I write the words and watch them pass
But, read it once, a brook is seen
The second time, a silken screen
'Tis magic of a different kind
My soul's far depths are intertwined
I paint the life with bright precision
And cast a spell of passioned vision
It sparkles at the fingertips
I spark a star, the words eclipse
At times the meaning's buried deep
I wade in far from shores too steep
I recognize the coral reef
It stands out now in bas-relief
But, look again, and it is gone
The firefly's light on summer's lawn
Or, like a glance at autumn's dawn
I sketch the tale, with charcoal drawn
For, now, such massive beauty there
Is rendered bright with massive care
And now, at last, a moment's peace
The words are laid, a short surcease

The Rhyme

The past is gone, where did it go?
There's nothing left but afterglow
To shine unto the soul of nights
And cast away all winter frights
When time has come and we must go
There's nothing left but afterglow
Where sun shines on in glowing view
There's nothing left to wear but you
So shrug it off, like last year's morph
Just blow and scoff, this strange, white dwarf
For anytime I need more rhyme
Just take a toss with scandaled time
And, just this once with giant shout
It's once around and twice devout
So solemnly I swear the vow
That's deeply spent with pensive brow

Transform

The power in all beauty and the honour of the soul
Will build the life to something well beyond the keeper's toll
Fling out the hand and toss a spell to raise the life at stakes
The clouds upon horizon speak and wonders what it wakes
The power in the Traveler will stand the test of time
So deep within the magic to transform the world in rhyme
As steps of thunder rock the world to bring the final fates
Stretch out the willing hand to her, the heart no longer waits
No tolerance is left here for the shirking and denial
It's time to rise above the past, transform this lifeless trial

Daunting Realms

At daunting coast, the challenge raves
'Tween cliffs of wrath and raging waves
The storm does toss within the sound
As raindrops splatter to the ground
The coast is reached, at last, so sure
The cliffs are scaled, now bright verdure
Are seen as far as eye can see
'Mid roaming beasts and vaulting tree
A path is spied along the way
With twists and turns where many stray
And, further on, more paths are strewn
Unending ways, discovered soon
Some, dark and dim, some filled with lust
Some bright and shining through the dust
Far distant crystal spires are seen
As dragons, jade, fly in between
The roar of dragons shakes the dust
You pause the beat, the seasons must
You'll need your courage as you find
Your way through daunting realms of mind
So staunch the will that reckons clear
Through bouts of doubt and silent tear

Warrior king

The warrior king sits on his throne
And, finds himself, once more, alone
His war was not with shield and sword
But, with the icy stream and ford
Of life and will and time and heart
Most wrenching struggle one can start
But, once it starts, one can't be faint
But boldly lose the least restraint
Into the fray with heart so strong
And, with a will and warrior's song

Dragon's paw

The dragon's paw does swat the pest
Tail lashes out and gives no rest
The dragon's eye says it's a test
So bold and brave, is he the best?
No fear is seen of Dragon's roar
The face is bright, the mind is more
No thunder, anger, roar, or paw
Compares to pain that he once saw
"Don't frighten me, you well-grown lizard
I've battled through time's fiercest blizzard
And, you can never be the end
You'll rant and roar, I'll lightly fend
Don't bother me with all your boast
Your fire will turn, and you will roast
So, drink with me, this merry toast
Of life and time, we'll make the most
I may ride you, you won't ride me
Let's to the mountain where we'll see
All lands below the wind as one
All people shining in the sun"
The dream is real, I feel it true
The Dragon's paw is there with you
The mailed fist pounds the mountaintop
To shake the land, the pain to stop
"Your Dragon's paw should fear this fist
Your tail, in anger, I might twist
No fear in me is left for you
You, Dragon's life, we're finally through"

Tossed Salad

I was feeling kinda gloomy while thinking 'bout a ballad
Some craziness had left me lone like bits of fresh tossed salad
I spent too long in seeking out some specious piece of valid
I found it buried oh so deep in, yes, you guessed ... tossed salad
Before the turn, I'd looked too close and found I was quite pallid
But, good, for now the pale is gone, and so is the tossed salad

Deep in thought

I contemplate the endless dreams
So deep in thought on all that seems
My mind on fire with all the life
Where do I lose all stress and strife
The singing of the wind along with sighing of the sea
Did bring, once more, the memory of all that life can be

The puzzle

Each day I pull the puzzle out to see just where I stand
Solve the riddle, find the clue, see where the pieces land
And, in a day, there's so much change, to take the breath away
I spend one day and brightened night, to find the piece to play
Curiouser and curiouser, I find it all to be
For from the heart and out the mouth, remains of what I see
Some days, the whole thing seems so clear, all answers to decree
And, then, a poof, they pop their top and all is gone, they flee
I scratch my head, once more, in thought, it's there and, then, it's gone
And, what of all that silliness I danced upon the lawn
There may be more within that dance than all those thoughts so deep
So, skip that silly pensive brow before it makes me weep
The pitter-patter of the rain, the soft brush of the snow
Its simple answers hold more truth than I will ever know

Mirrors

Dedicated to Katie Belle
The mirror holds a magic
The words just set it free
Whether bold or tragic
The eyes just let it see

Shatterfall

Shatterfall, the wind too weary
From crowds encumbered there
Alone the darkness, sad and bleary
The crowds too large to care
The crowds still gather, grow each day
So many lost along the way
As fame fools some and glory too
The clamors rise in grayish hue
All inspirations lost to din
The heart decides to seek within
For fame and glory, only slew
Drives sanity through depth to true
But, now, the teeming masses whole
Amass the silence of the soul
Wherefore, the soul cries out its heart
To find the way and, then, the start
Soul sings such songs as wills the ways
Eyes closed, heart opens, body sways
Then, follows there, in comfort dark
Vast shining vistas, sere and stark
For now is seen the vain false hope
Of crowds that teem on broken slope
But way is seen beyond the dearth
It's seen to be pure, fallow earth
And further on is seen the field
That only seeds of soul can yield
No longer lost to touch and feel
No longer tossed, the soul is healed
It lies all 'round, soul can't confirm
But guides eternity to term

Room full of mirrors

I wandered through a room so full of mirrors
It showed the life and will just so much clearer
Than ever seen before
Each one reflects a different trace
Such different views, familiar face
To help to find the core
Who is this man that stands so proud
What is that shadow-looking shroud
Behind one face shows gems and stones
Bold sparkles glint from shadowed thrones
Each glass reflects a lesson taught
With lines and aches that life had wrought
The grimness seldom left a mark
For heart would not provide the spark
To settle for much less than joy
One still can see the little boy
But, oh, so slowly, see the man

Smoking embers

Smoking embers flair to flame
While mind disintegrates the same
Explosions rock the very core
Just shattered remnants from before
Are cast, once more, upon the table
Along with what is left of fable
The storied eyes that see the heart
And slowly watch it break apart
The smallest piece, so fresh and clean
The likes of which are seldom seen
So slow to reach, unsteady hand
To place them slowly back, again
The slowest sigh from deepest core
That straightens back for life, once more

The final say

To wake up every day and dream while through this life we walk
To step beyond the doldrums, visions through the eyes we talk
A world without remorse
It takes its final course
To launch a view
My heart in you
And, in that heart, no fearful start, no message there to balk
Come flying through the winds of change as steeply as a hawk
I did stand tall, this life to live
With beauty rich, my heart to give
This one stands tall and to the one
For next, we step beneath the sun
As rivers tear away the flood
The ripples wash away the blood
Like trees all standing in a row, no break in line, no fault
Far tossed away, all bitterness, the cruel and fey does halt
The rippled dreams
And smoothest seams
All hearts as one
Beneath the sun
Imagine this, with sweetest kiss, into the dream we vault

The wonder

A special world of wonder that is written in the mind
When looking close within, you'll see it's there for all to find
Rampaging days, the fire is bright
The gloom pushed back with endless light
As blasting forth, all rockets flare
And bring a light to all who dare

Kingdom

The battered crown on golden throne does lie
Upon the wall, heraldic sign of sky
The doors to Hall swing wide, in stride's the mountain king
The sword in hand of might of which he holds as if to fling
But settles on his throne with pensive brow
Through ages gone he sees the where and how
What will to hold so steady to the course
To save his people from the least remorse

The fire in the mind

Look out below, he shouts too slow
The fire in mind's about to blow
The smoke has billowed all day long
The wind has fanned the flames too strong
The earth does shake, I feel it now
That final singe upon the brow
I hear the rumble to the bone
This time the blast will move the throne

Foreign lands

The mind is shattered on the rocks thrown up by foreign shore
Unsure of acts, the heart now stands and rises to the fore
On foreign lands, on hobbled legs, look out upon the sea
Remember there, with fondest thoughts, a distant memory
The will to stumble forward, now, upon the distant coast
Is something few have had the will to later have the boast

Dreamscape

I walk, today, within a world that no one else will see
I step on through the bounds of dream while walking 'round a tree
And, on the other side, the crystal rainbows 'cross the sky
The bridges built of tears, no longer linger in the eye
The rays of sun wash all the smiles to bright
The hearty sing with all their heart and might
The beauty rings upon the throne
That's built of heart in perfect tone
Upon the throne sits, in her glory
Most wondrous being told in story
There's glitter on her gown
Pure gems upon her crown
Shot through with light and ringing sound
The universe was surely bound
Upon her brow, she'd wait of years
Still burdened by the weight of tears
So lightly, did she raise her form
Transcendent night, like bridled storm
Far past horizon did she gaze
All living hearts did slowly raise
In bravest hopes that she would find
The one the story surely signed
Her heart did sing a lovely tune
As, boldly, sun did break to noon
And all the wonders of the land
Slowly passed beneath my hand
As I laid down my pen

Dreamland

Look out upon the waves of light as they rush over me
Trembling fine to crave delight in all I do and see
No sprite or elf has such a dance as prances through my mind
Day in, day out, the beauty sprouts for something's there to find
A bauble, dido, smile, or quirk is hidden in each niche
Explore until the end of time, this story that is rich
The beauty bound between our souls, knows all about the sighs
And sings a note, so hard to reach, it splits the sparkling skies
Prepare, for here it comes again, to cleanse the vacant room
So, with a whirl and sprightly step, the soul does swing the broom
For, after all, each one shall seek their way on through the copse
To wonderfields of everlasting sighs, and joys, and hopes

The Forest floor

or, Metamorphosis of all you knew

Wrap the thought, like all the rest, with bounds of gentle care
In life and love and glory felt, that shows the will to share
A deep, untroubled sleep is spent, a pause in all that's thought
The steep and final leap is lent to laws for all that's wrought
The mist it lifts from forest floor revealing autumn day
A shaft of light, through limbs and leaves, bequeaths the final ray
Before the silk is spun in place to close the life before
No glimmer, hint, nor slightest sense, holds breath for so much more
Hung from branch of patience spent, so long the winter day
The beauty on the wing of reason, now comes into play

Threshold

Within the mind, the silence grows and softens all the winds
The echoes off the canyon walls of whiteness so begins
A tale of wanderings in length, the surety absurd
The deepness of the forest, now, precludes a single word
The way is deep and meaningful, the darkness only right
But, as you cross that threshold bare, the meaning only light
To wiggle out a word or two, the meaning for the drums
The vista, now, so clear and bright, the song within you thrums
No time for tides or willanuck, the very air you breathe
Brings sense of life, momentous thrust, upheave all thoughts and seethe
The end and the beginning, now, are finally in sight
The end of all that one has known, transformed to what is right

moss and bark

I trickle past the winding bells that ring, again, so true
And wash away the sands of time, held closely by so few
And, at the stop
Right near the top
I fly on home to you
But, then, again, I spend the sun on wondrous swirling view
And, find, beneath the moss and bark that, here, is sterling too

Now until end of winter

From now until end of winter is my time to write
With words, like arms, arrayed, once more, so surely filled with might
The pulse of heart transcribed
It stands foremost in battlefield of comprehension's war
As how to understand this life, that bursts with so much more
When will of life's imbibed
The words were trained to celebrate, amazed at such a chore
The glory of the days and years, with all of life in store
The seasons, cycles, clocks that tick, the rhythm of the heart
That pulse like wildness on the wind and blows the door apart
Now, look within the workings of eternity's own space
And see beyond the stanza's rhyme, beyond the moment's race
The shining helm and lance and sword of verse are now on guard
Alone, they stand upon their strength, within the hallowed yard
To guard the very door of time from shatterfall without
With practiced will of reasoned strength, they guard the last redoubt

Reflections

I wander through a windowed way
Where each reflection has its say
Of what is left and what is done
Of where and how the tale is spun
The simplest pleasures do entail
Reflections from the windows pale
Just look on through and what you'll see
Is tinkers hammers breaking free
On through that room, next window see
Reflections there of you and me
And, through that window, nothing more
For in that room, lies opened door
To what's unseen with true delight
Reflection, now, of your own light

Poems

Kaleidoscope of images that circle all around
The eye that looks into the heart, seeks something to be found
A sparkle here, a flash of blue, a brightness bent to fit
A mark is scratched, a fastness gone by all the ones that lit
Awaiting for their time to come and bounce so brightly done
The elves sit in their trees and wait to stage their sprightly fun
And, with a will to make things clear of masked intent and need
Within a poem all is seen and heart is gladly freed

Ripples on the wind

Scattered sparks fly to the sky
The night is ripped, the wind yells fie
The frozen tundra welcomes me
The end of all will never be
Protest the bend too sharply done
Embrace the life when finally run
The weyr is high, the wind is near
That day is bright, the breath is clear
Upon the way where minstrels try
And, soar on back to heart from sky
The mountains breathe a smoky sigh
Wings open wide, hearts, once more, fly

The will of the wind

The will of the wind has something to say
When it comes to the bending of trees
But, think what you will, at the end of the day
Mankind should not bend as it please
It's nonsense to think and throw up one's hand
Behaviour, so clear, unbecoming of man
The triggers are set, we run just like mice
Without the least thought, not once, deuce, but thrice
Now, dignity's armour will come to the fore
And bring down the house so littered and sore

The will of the wind 2

The will of the wind has something to say
When it comes to the bending of trees
But, think what you will, at the end of the day
Mankind should not bend as it please
It's nonsense to think and throw up one's hand
Behaviour so clearly unbecoming of man
The triggers are set, we run just like mice
Without the least thought, we run for the spice
Now, dignity's armour will come to the fore
And bring down the house and make of it more
The glitter is seen as all sparkly and nice
But, now it is seen, that it's worth less than rice
The will of the wind will be lost, at the last
The bending of will, just a thing of the past

Moire'

When all the wind is at your will
With toss of hand, all life stands still
A nod of head will bend the ray
And, broken blade will enter fray
To travel on the course to end
No drift to left nor right does wend
No way in which to fail the test
Each step is rich, each touch is best
To trickle down the craggy break
And, in one's heart, the patterns take
The spirit's moire' shimmers faint
And, life moves on without the taint

Endings

The walls, they crept, while glance was gone
The time it took is lost to dawn
The brightness shields the eyes from pain
The glory sometimes seems to wane
No end to all that's come and gone
False sense of endings is the pawn
In all the life, in all that's true
Beginnings gone and endings new

Wonderfall

I trip a time across the sky
All life, to me, does call
I'm learning, slowly, how to fly
I stumble, wonderfall
In honor of the Fairy Queen
Bow down within her hall
The sparkling water, seldom seen
We watch the wonderfall
'Tis time of sense, the heart relents
The Traveler must stand tall
To see beyond the broken bents
'Fore leaping wonderfall
I dive on in, a giant leap
And, to the birds I call
Cascading water, far and deep
I dive from wonderfall

Rhythms of Life

The rhythms of this life are such they need not look profound
The seasons, tides, the night and day, moon's phases so resound
They sneak up close, without a glance
And stay to welcome rhythm's dance
The universe is singing though you may not hear it yet
Each star, my heart, is singing to the rhythm we have set

Incarnations

An incarnation, long ago, I played the royal strife
And, then, the mask changed in its view
To tinker on with life
But, days do change, both me and you
And, all the days are rife
With wonders in the meadow lands and twirls of pixie dust
We wander through far distant lands, and brush away the rust
The wind moves on, the stars align, the wonders never cease
And, in this wonderland of all, we find eternal peace

Head up

My wanderings have traveled far, with, seldom, clear intent
The message sent in bottle's keep is seldom simply sent
The thorns and thickets battled through, are deep and sharply walled
So often, the exploring is turned back and clearly stalled
Distractions in the syllabus will never go away
Along with brief unpleasantness, not difficult to stray
Mountains hurdle in the way, to boldly crest the view
Oceans separate the times, left simply to the few
To trudge along is not the case, high stepping is still due
Just snap the heels, ignore the thorns, and onward to be true

Juggernaut

The thunder heart is far away
But, getting closer every day
The rails they shake, the dust it flies
The rumble through the earth, but cries
"The juggernaut is on his way"
All sounds just stop, as if a stay
Of execution were performed
And, all the world informed
The wildest ride you've ever known
It bucks and screams in scaling tone
The mountains shudder, move away
The juggernaut has come to stay

The perfect storm

So seldom worlds collide in perfect storm
In boldest type as well as willing form
All broken, shattered, left for endless pale
Tremendous will with spokes that sometimes fail
The geysers rumble at the winded marks
The flaming seas give way to glacial sparks
The thunder rooted deeply in the stem
Of life and brutal thoughts of wicked meme
For flaring stars reel back from final fate
On broken wings that flail and sadly bate

Grand

It stands outright, in regal sense, with loyalist proportions
It sings a note of recompense that's lost in the distortions
A sparkle there, is littered here, and, with it, goes the sky
Bright moon sends shadows round the scarp evoking winsome cry
To seize upon the windlass sheet and pull with all your might
No crush will craze the troubled heart from tears of sudden sight
Swing out upon the windlass' rope and sweep onto the fore
Reach far above the mast to sky, beyond the ocean's roar
You'll sway into the lunar light of pinnacle's repine
For bursting forth from shadow's depth will come the grand design

Realms of amazement

My mind is shattered by the times and by the tales I've told
Through ages and the augury, deep shards these eyes behold
My breath, I catch, from time to time, as all goes whizzing by
With blinding light I see so clear and, then, so nearly fly
Transcendent, now, the will as one, the strength is of the heart
The trials still come, the tests won't end, if life, you still take part
A juggernaut, I think myself, I too, go whizzing by
The blinding light, I see so clear, sometimes I nearly fly

Whickwithy

The Treehouse

Welcome to the treehouse mansion
Where the tree becomes the stanchion
Sturdy life, it grows in strength
Far beyond the platform's length
Through branches wide the house will flow
Up and out from life the love will grow
The leaves that ease the Summer's heat
In winter, leaves, Sun's warmth won't meet
Upon the eaves, watch life burst free
When, once, you build upon a tree
It holds you in its arms so wide
The structure seems to burst with pride
Without or with prosodic scansion
Welcome to the tree house mansion

Transformation

Cloudy skies and caterpillars harken to the norm
All seems so calamitous until we've reached the storm
All fractals scattered to the winds, how real the life can be
And, never once to touch the ground in distant memory
For when the storm has struck
And, we have tried our luck
The crystal skies and butterflies
Will swirl beyond the crippled tries
The storm no longer waiting
No time for moderating
The churning sea and broken lee
No longer call to you and me
For gentle lea of life to be
We are the ones, at last, will see
All seasons and the reasons stand beyond the windswept norm
With butterflies and rainbows spewing from the falling storm
The storm that never broached the rail
Calamity that never failed
That self-bent honesty

Thoughts

So sad, they speak coincidence
So dulled by life's experience
So conquered by man's great façade
So numbed to Nature's simple nod
There's more to life than chug and shake
It is a dance, make no mistake
To drudge through life from stem to stern
With nothing left and nothing learned
So, to my heart, I now commit
To find the time and so, to wit
Not hasten to the vain and glory
But, find my own true life and story
Up from the depths of furthest past
Upon my future life, I cast
It is no gamble, though may seem
To ride upon bold time's own stream
For this is what it's all about
It is but life's most bold redoubt
To know, so deep, that I am one
With all of time, within I've won
To hold the love and find the peace
This battled soul will never cease
To understand this peace I glimpse
My wearied soul, along it limps
It is the peace of soul, I say
'Tis not the peace of one bright day
For battles will be fought and lost
For peace of soul, there is a cost
So, 'til this war is lastly won
I glory now, beneath the sun
I know it's hard to understand
It often seems like shifting sand
And, when I reach the age of dust
Will I still hold this final trust?
Yes

Await the day
Here I sit, await the day
Too early up, no more to say
There's nothing open, tide is high
There's naught to do, a different sigh
And, still await the day
Still dark outside

Synergist
Like strings upon a puppet
Or threads within a web
They pull together up it
But, synthesize instead
Like leaves and branches on a tree give stunning strength to fit
The synthesis, like magic born, when you lean intuit
When all the threads align
And synergies combine
There never is an end to it
When learning of the intuit

imagineers
Sudden thought struck hard today upon creative force
As lightning strikes across the sky, imagineers will source
The beauty of the word and wit
But, even more, the form and fit
The confidence you wield so lightly comes from deep within
Each step you take approaches bliss, much closer to a win
Sometimes the force of worlds will battle on through every step
You carry on, with all your strength, completing one more rep
The beauty of the written word so subtly doubles down
When written from the force to write, there is no need to frown
That force that's so creative clearly growing all the while
New wit, new script, new song to write, all confidence and smile
I do it for myself, today, I do it with a smile

Guidance

What of the guide we always seek
From birth unto our death
Without, the future can seem bleak
We can't just hold our breath
Whate'er we find that shows the way
We sense so surely brighter day
And celebrate the time
So rest, this day, your wearied bones
And sing, no more, in shattered tones
For clarity's sublime

Passersby

Just a part of the landscape
Just a snap, apart it breaks
We pass on through as lives escape
The song gives back that which it takes
No more than just some scenery
To entertain a passer-by
Like loveliness of greenery
It makes heart beat and gently sigh
The beauty is a wonder
And, of that there is no doubt
Mid clash of light and thunder
As the inside has come out
What makes me different from a tree
The awe with which all that I see
The wonders that surround
It now will pass, no more to be
I drive on deep into the sea
Of molecules around

Everlast

Stray stars streak through my mind and pass
With soft impressions, Everlast
Unto my mind is given thought
On all that is and all that's wrought
The periled depths both new and bold
So fill my mind to end the cold
To take the chill from unknown paths
Gain summer's warmth in Everlast
And, as my spring accepts its winter
The mind shall know and not be hindered
Just as my future routs the past
I'm off, again, to Everlast
A golden, open breezy field
Within this dream, my fate is sealed
Oh, Lady Luck, you're cards, don't deal
For Luck is not the sword I wield
Defense is open-armed, I clasp
All patience gained from Everlast
Fantastic as this thought may be
I now, and well, can clearly see
'Tis but a part that's but a start
For, now, alone, so stands the Art
Away, again, so neighs the heart
Bright wondrous fields that never part
For all that's seen and all that's past
Is only part of Everlast

Images of last resort

The young will always start with hope and purest of intentions
The wit then comes to break apart all life's most fond conventions
Of fashioning, and fancy dress, what of all pomp and styles
Though time will wash away with tidal wave of childhood smiles
Engaged in dancing of the spheres, the swirling nature's taunts
There comes alive in all of this the loving avalanche

The drum

For when the time has finally come
Of longer shadows, fading drum
And every beat of drum and heart
So slowly gains the leading part
Of every moment's thought
Does life become more precious?
Each moment more infectious
With love and laughter for this life?
Or droll with dread and dreary strife?
What is so dearly bought?
When does this life, in fact, begin?
With bleating on the endless wind?
When first we burst upon this earth
All raucous from our recent birth?
Is that the moment caught?
Or when this life and love we grasp
With every moment, cause to gasp
At life's so many fickled ways
And revel in the tricks she plays
That life has never taught?
When does this life begin to end?
When body stops, no more to mend?
Or, when the heart no longer cares
And, when the mind no longer spares
Some time for reveled thought?
I was born the other day
Though many years had gone their way
I did not live until that time
Those many years without a rhyme
Were poorly sold and bought
I'll live this life, each moment comes
Each heartbeat rival to the drums
No longer will I wile the wait
Delayed unto some moment great
I'll waste a moment not
Now, feel the drumbeat of the life
Don't wait upon a moment rife

So full of patience and denial
As if it were some endless trial
So full of endless rot
And, if I live another day
No longer will I let it stray
From life adorned until the time
That I no longer will the rhyme
And dance, the lady caught
When does life end, you might well ask
When life becomes an endless task
Without an end in mindless sight
And on and on, an endless fright!
I shudder at the thought
No, dead is not the end of things
Nor death the dirge whose ending brings
Forth all the waste upon this earth
Now, here, beside the frozen firth
Break open to the spot
Where seas of love can well be found
Where life is bold and well renowned
For 'tis the will that leads the way
To endlessly bring love and play
And, that is what I've got
She is the thought that's bold and free
With fiercest love, she anchors me
To all of life's rare sweetest blessings
And all its lovely, wondrous dressings
Beyond the slightest doubt
There is no more to life than that
Let's speak no more of kit and kat
So, well upon this tireless way
I revel now and I do say
It is of love I spout
Oh, tally up the tender sums
Life echoes to the beat of drums
That pound along the endless way
As if each beat did clearly say
We are still here and stout
And dally more if that's your will

Each beat a pulse to cause a thrill
Each breath a song to always fill
The heart no longer sitting still
Each moment to the top
And, still along the way I go
To toss the hammer, bell the blow
The hammer do I surely throw
The bell is there so that I know
Just at the end full stop

The depths

And, now, so deep into the soul we go
The swirling tug confesses undertow
It's when we reach the depths, so placid down
See what sits on throne in shining crown
What reigns in there to save the soul, not break
What wanders there to brace the goals we make
Converse there of the partings on the lawn
And pass a cup of tea from dusk to dawn
Let leaves now linger on the thoughts we make
And strings be strummed for all the thoughts we take
We live the moment if it is to live
And, with that toast, will of the moment give
For destiny is all that we shall see
When written well upon jubilee

Guidance, second version

Where is that guide we always seek
From birth on to our death
Without, the future can seem bleak
We can't just hold our breath
Whate'er we find to show the way
We sense so surely brighter day
And celebrate the sign
So rest, this day, your wearied bones
And, sing, no more, in shattered tones
For clarity's divine

The life and times

Through It all, time ebbs and flows
And, with it all, our life, it goes
But, what, if not a passing fact
Our life went on, in full, in tact
The children always know so much
But, time, Oh Time! They never touch
As gentle as a summer breeze
Time passes by, among the trees
A leaf, it falls and settles down
It then cascades, an autumn mound
So time now ticks with every sound
Another leaf, another round
The hearse is rolling toward the town
Our gaze is fixed as though it's found
The end of all, clear, sharp, and final
That breaks the nerve and snaps the spinal
But, who can see beyond the veil
What sight would see, if walls we scale
The heart, the heart, can only know
What lies beyond the endless flow
Of time and death, we cringe and quake
Approaching our relentless wake
The life is lost, pursuit's pure folly
The heart, the heart must guide the trolley
Only hills that hide the trail
Beyond the hills, goes on the rail
No magic world need be defined
Our hearts, our hearts become refined
So shake the terror from the soul
For time is one and we are whole
As time does fade into facade
Life's no joke, give time no nod

Immediatement

Look deep into the prism's soul
And watch the light that enters whole
So, passing through, the light still shines
But transcends colors, crystal tines
The whitest light that meets the core
Transforms itself to shards galore
With just a fraction, time can make
It's all so changed when life's at stake
So, twinkle for a little while
Embrace it all, do life with style

Ripples in time

The ripples in time, they cascade along
Building on each other
The grand design grows much too strong
With strength, they strike and smother
The giant and the small
Together see the fall
So great it's like a lover

The crowded sea

A double take I had to make when once I found the tale
"How could it break", I sudden spake, "without it ending pale"
The manic and the frenzy sweeping through the crowded sea
It suddenly made sense, at last, when standing by the lee
The soothing and the calm I'd felt within the sheltered rocks
But crowd just followed one on one from life within the lochs
I stood the test when battered best by sanity's own plea
Dichotomy of dreams and life did fall to ash, you see
No slightest wisp of wave succeeding wave
Did ever cross this simple mind to save

Whickwithy

Sway

I enter on the balcony above the royal hall
And, as I gaze upon the guests, I think, once more, "Stand tall!"
That is the way to start the dance, the only dance that counts
'Tis with a will and with the strength to sway with swing and bounce
From life to life, no more the thought that ever wind will raise
The spectre of that struggle gone along with its own maze
For time does take unto itself, at last, to rake and raze
But, deep inside the endless soul looks on with steady gaze

The joy of life

The joy of life, so gently done
Whichever path beneath the sun
Must not miss out on all the fun
Let revel shout and others stun
For Double entendre's not a pun
In glades and fields we've always run
Don't wear a frown, they weigh a ton
The lightened heart already won

Open Wide

I spread my arms out opened wide, lean back, I fall into
The open arms of life that hold me close and pass me through
To open, warm and gentle arms of loving in this life
No need, I find, to cringe away, facades are all the strife
Like stepping stones upon a pond, that stand above the wave
And save me from a drowning end, life's arms are all I crave
All nature brings me closer to the feel for such a way
And, never far from nature will you ever see me stray
But, nature, all alone, can only be there for so much
Above the waves, upon the stones, one craves the human touch

Crystal clear

As life progresses through a stage and time goes on its way
The complex weave comes crystal clear, like brightness lightens day
No need, no point to sacrifice a single honesty
Within the age, through crystal bright, a sight all life should see
The sheltered heart looks out upon a life with all the best
The will that matches sheltered heart withstands the whirlwind test
The crystal clearly shining now
To light the solemn, final vow
The will now takes the whicker lamp
The crystals shine on mankind's ramp
Of real achievement's man will do
The crystal's light now shines on through

Silences

The quiet of an evening
The stardreams of a night
The silent soul that's singing
The heart that glows with light
The silence of a dawning as it turns from grey to green
All life is at a pause in time until all eyes have seen
The sadness of a soul that's lost upon their lonely way
The joy when soul comes back, again, to light the brightest day
The gaze from eye to eye that goes between the two that love
The gaze upon the numinous and bluest sky above
The silence in a heart for one where brightness once had been
And, all the silence of a world, not heard, but sometimes seen

Trusting life

Sometimes it's hard to hold onto a thorough faith in life
Sometimes it's shaken by the winds of change and human strife
There really isn't any need for struggles as we live
We should accept eternity in all in which to give
Our heart to all and sundry for the sweet expanse of all
Arms and heart out opened wide, no longer fear the fall

Gaia

She came into this world alone
Child of heart but fully grown
And walked along the ridge of stone
Full of heart, but nothing known
Not knowing whence or where she came
Not even knowing of her name
But then a light and gentle touch
A heart of light that means so much
Wherefrom the sigh of love and such
In such a world as this bright ball
Love should surely conquer all
But on its flickering way it went
To come again, when heaven sent
But just, for now, the way is rent
So, with a sigh, she stands unbent
And, with that sigh, a strength is lent
A task awaits, a time unspent
"Why am I here?", she shouts aloud
No one replies, but hears the crowd
The glistened way is all in shroud
Too deep the turmoil has been plowed
Of concrete things, we were so proud
No things of heart were then allowed
All mankind so surely cowed
Upon the grasping, man had bowed
She gazed out, then, upon the endless ocean
Passion caught within unceasing motion
Rocks and ocean all around
Her destiny as yet unfound
Upon the rocks, her destiny
She meets her love to be set free
His blood pumps through her heart to fold
The deepest bond our kind can hold
They stand upon the rocky point
All alone, their souls anoint
Eternity with waves unbound
Something new is finally found

They look upon the world as new
Hand in hand, the leaf and dew
From there, beginning had begun
Wave on wave beneath the sun
Life goes on as all will say
Reckoned to this very day
A tendrilled thought reached out so kind
Those touched were thought to lose their mind
John, of regal industry
Engaged a beggar to be free
Jim, the spouse of angered core
His wife, he found now, to adore
Within the fewest spanning days
Big Pharma dreamed of TLAs
Winding, writhing so in vain
She harkened to the utter pain
What of this world that's gone insane
When will they learn, a slight restrain
Joe's free spirit, bent and twisted
Puppy's eyes, so full and misted
Brought the flood of unknown tears
Hidden by a life of fears
White fury blazed beyond her knowledge
As she entered power's college
She went to face the power's core
Beyond all fear, they did ignore
To the guns, the leader nods
With narrowed eyes, she breaks the odds
Bullets into flowers from the rifles' stems of pods
"I could bend your minds, so doing, break
So inflexible did you finally make
Your heart and all about you
No thought remaining true
Shed it now, I warn you once
Or you will pay it in the nonce
With pompousness within their eyes
Few of that ilk believed her cries
And, pay they did, in endless coin
All wit was lost and thought disjoined

The epidemic spread worldwide
Setting free a rising tide
As Empathy and passion fiercely rose
So arrogance came quickly to a close
Only the worst of minds were broken
Softly done and seldom spoken
And, as transition took its place
Tears ran down her loving face
They stood, again, upon the rocks
No time left, now, to save from shocks
"My darling, dear, my time is run
I've faced the tide, it all is done
And, now, I can no longer stay
But, darling!" She cried, "I'll miss your way!"
Tears streamed down in deep remorse
Her life did seem to run its course
Her body limp as death will do
No movement left and lips of blue
His head bowed down in anguished pain
His tears poured down like unleashed rain
But, wait! she stirs within his arms
How can this be? what are the charms?
She looks into his eyes and smiles
"Have I fallen by a while?"
"You said that you must now move on
Change your mind, my loving one?"
"Where am I now, I'm sorry, sir
I know you not, but some things stir
As if I knew, another time
As if we were a loving rhyme"
"Yes, my darling, that is true
All I'll say is I love you
And hope, again, you'll love me too
As time does pass to see us through
I'll wait until you know it's true
Because, my darling, I love you"
The love is showing in her face
As she says, "No need to pace
For I can feel it now, and it is surely true

That, yes, in fact, there is no doubt that I indeed love you
The feeling is as adamant as if 'twere cast in stone
That I will never leave your side nor ever be alone
As long as I am here with you
For I know your love is true
'Twill last through age unknown
I know as cast in stone"
As Gaia spread throughout the world
The words were sighed by just a girl
The sigh that breaths of love

The program

Tick-tock goes the clock
In computer's heart
IF a smile THEN show all style
AND Happy program start
GOTO dreams, IF heart is seen
AND what it seems is pure and clean
THEN GOTO revel's part
ELSE....well, never mind

A cozy little life

I dream so often, while I wake, a cozy little life
A cozy little slice of time without the slightest strife
A chimney through the middle and stone house to snuggle all
The evergreens and flowers, vines, and wooded path do call
A peaceful glen, that's hid so well, at end of wooded path
It silences all human din, as nature has a bath
A smile creeps in, the laughter's sound
The eyes so bright, light heart is found
A little walk, a little ways, as shores wash to the sea
The murmur of the ocean lulls the past of history
And, here, I find myself, at last
No more the wind, no more the past
Around the tree, the die is cast

The sea of life

The wind picked up and flew upon the sail
Soul brightened as the east began to pale
The sound of billows leapt across the sky
We tacked the ship to give this life a try
The wind broke free, the tempest roared and flailed
That roaring sound of heart that nearly failed
The waves that crashed so high as passions mount
Across the deck, it flings like wondrous fount
So smoothly moved along the wave's sharp crest
That, now, the sea has lastly come to rest
And, now, the languor soothes the savage sea
Horizons lost, no longer waves to be
As lost in time, there is no land in sight
And, yet, the sun, the breeze, feel, oh, so right
It's time, again, to run along the rail
Aweigh the anchor, raise so high the sail
For lands unknown lie far unto the fore
Let's ride the winds, again, to farthest shore

Lightning

The waves engender lightning as I struggle to the shore
I feel the shock of wind and rain, and don the helm, once more
The weight of salty water bears me, slowly, towards the ground
The strength of tides required now, to keep me safely bound
Upon a course set years ago
The footsteps set precise and slow
The flicker of the lightning brightens all the ways in which
The leaves of time will blow away, all seasons at a pitch
I drag myself above the tides, beyond the craggy crest
And stand above the highest rocks, for Traveler, a test
I turn and look upon the ocean's ragged, furied wake
As trav'ler, bending test of time, recovers from the ache

The challenge

Throughout this life and all the strife, the gauntlet must be run
Betwixt the smiles and bows and riles, betwixt all of the fun
The focused will, all fate to fill, is what I must implore
The clutters and the mutters are so easy to ignore
But, when a heart does sing a scale of similar intent
The peace, the view, the pale of new, so suddenly is rent
A baffled wave of shimmered masks are all that I could see
But, never in my heart have I been one who deigned to flee
So, face the haze as if all life were in the shimmering
And, bring the will round to the point to clear the glimmering
Oh, Bright one, scrutinize this point, and find the answer there
For has it changed or been confirmed and, yes, I deeply care
Another step along the way is meant for here and now
And, if this is too cryptic spoke, 'tis glimmer in the vow
The vow is not affected
The challenge is perfected
The haze, a little clearer still
Eternity goes on

The mystery of the Tapestry

Each day I marvel at the weaves of this wondrous tapestry
Declares itself like fall to leaves, on the binding registry
The needle runs both fore and aft, the thread is woven on the throw
So many threads, from heart and craft, each color lit by heart's own glow
Some, in a moment, captious free, leave behind some mystery
And, then, some few, so silently, come flying through your history
It's battened to the core
New shedding says there's more
To come
The kingdom's cloth is known by few, yet, markings show the last detail
The shuttle knows just what to do and stands the test of time and tale
Whither on the way we'll weave, a picture pure and clear or fell
And, all the tatters we will cleave, no tattered tale is this we tell

Whickwithy

And, once again, stand back and see the wondrous tale of tapestry
It gathers round you setting free and breathes life in like forestry
Your heart is at the fore
Its beat, hard to ignore,
The drum
When you need a taste of life
Or, build some strength from stress and strife
As gently done as love and lace
It builds so subtly at its pace
So like the answer hidden there
So plain to view, though one must stare
And look for subtleties of all
In cloth that's draped within the hall
If we forget to weave our web
And live the tapestry instead
Amazing thing this doom
That's flung along the loom
The warp is still and weft flies straight and through
With patience watch what artist's hand will do
In golden threads, the Arras' weave will be
Displayed in royal hall for all to see
The pattern one, no chance to recreate
So boldly hung, this canopy of state
This final scene is beautiful indeed
Displayed for all with heart that's finally freed
To see the weave and recognize its make
And, now, at last, eyes open wide, you wake

Brightness

Bright are the days, and long are the nights
Gentle the hand that soothes all the frights
With passion unhinged and heart that's awake
The brightness outshines, the balance at stake
When left to the woods, so leafless and bare
The world will revolve and bring us such care
Of life with a wind that bends the branch down
Like a mystery blow with the slightest of sound

The Dark

I'll never ignore the darkened pain
Nor shun the tale it spoke, again
The time has come to shout for joy
The torch is passed, with love employ
Oh, yes you were so very right
Not one will dare, you've fought your plight
America, now too, I'll sing
And hope for faith that you can bring
Your vision needed desperately
To wake the land of love you see
And break the bitter of despair
And break the tyrants, foul and bare
So, can your heart push on the fight
That flickers, now, for wrong and right
This race is worn unto the end
We pass the torch, your way to fend
High vistas, now, are opened wide
Your will shines through with regal pride
Beauty is as beauty does
Now, bring it home, twice written was

Friends

A friend is but a miracle of time, and fate, and need
A wonderment of wind and rain and, oft, unstated creed
A balance held, along the wire, of honour, thought, and deed
A bond complete, from nonce to nonce, with this the heart is freed
So tentative, like new-born chick, fresh from the eggshell flung
The balance held, for lifetime long, no better song is sung

Threnody

The blast is blown, I shrug it off
No need remorse, no need to scoff
But, agony I'll feel for you, if hurt is on your way
With threnody, I'll tilt the skew, my heart is here to stay
I will not tolerate the pain that has been given you
My blood pours out to salve your heart and wash the troubled view
When pain is gone and heart is strong, come rest your weary head
We'll talk of soaring eagles' wings and Cheshire cats, instead

Balance

I lost my balance long ago, but wobbled on through time
With staggerdrop, I played along, the reason for the rhyme
Was in the depths of deepest past, I walk along the way
Head bent down, the thought of rhyme, no way in which to stray
The pressure on the deepest run was always there for me
The way in which the shadows run, please hear my shattered plea
The turn, in fact, was written, once, with brightest feathered tip
And, once again, the balance kept and nectar slowly sip

Winter nights

The seasons have all come and gone
No longer any form of fawn
So, back to winter, once again
The life moves on from what has been
The days are shorter, now, by far
The crisper air to view the star
A sigh creeps up to frosty breath
To prove I have not met my death
I am not frozen in this stance
Just gazing stars with brightened glance

Waves too

The susurration of the waves has washed ashore a thought
The cresting waves surfed thru the heart & peace & love were wrought
Insanity had had its reign, upon a lower shelf
Replaced with clefs within the soul-etched score that sings of self
Insights of life are sometimes scribed throughout the spanning years
Hard fought to find, sometimes those lessons etched with well-worn tears
I know the youth will scoff at this, there's nothing there to learn
To save, just one, from all that painful waste and useless burn
For as the waves, so joyous, wash away all of the grime
I find upon the shore's bright sand the glitter and the rhyme
Embracing life, in deeper pools, not ripples in the tide
Those superficial textures disappear like sandy stride
I settle on the sand as lowest tide sweeps in return
And, watch the waves of stellar light blast forth in steady burn
The moon shines forth, and stars portray the spark in all that's been
Of life and love and passion found and all the beauty seen
The waves of sound, from thundrous notes, begin and end the score
A wave of light, or is it tide, shakes cosmos to the core

Devastation

Devastation has, once more, crashed deep into my life
Here, once more, the windless core, brings pain to heart, so rife
The will is paid upon the stone but words be broken tools
Left alone, the faults lie prone, like herd of lonely fools

Unreserved love

It's maybe just my nature to give all I have to give
How does one feel at all, if so reservedly they live
A stinginess, indeed, if all the heart I cannot throw
So,. off the precipice, once more, full braced for where I go
Along the drop and not a single bone is, thus so, broke
But, heart, it flies and breath is caught, the dream has been awoke
So, dream with me and make this world a better place to live
And, come with me and we will give what's possible to give

Fractals

Those fractals of the forest and along the seashore line
Don't say you understand this life, that runs along so fine
No more the fractals on the wind can ever be confined
Away, upon the saddened thought, we seek the random blind
We pass away to stardust now, for on the brink we sit
As if a puzzle to the sun, our single species fit
To test the stream upon the burst, a flashing, brightened source
The cosmic wind is building, serendipity's on course
Don't let the wash across the sky bring blue to have a taint
Don't let your heart look at the stars and fall away in faint

Crippled tongue

With broken heart and crippled tongue, the way in which you smile
Not lifeless heart or shattered tombs can make me feel so vile
As if I broke upon the rocks, bones crumble down to dust
The doors and wheels just fall apart, give way to crumbled rust
But, once again, I grit my teeth and up I rise, once more
I take a sigh and break the smile to see what's still in store

The shore

I walk along the rocky shore
My thoughts go out to sea, once more
I pause upon the seaward course
I wish to trust without remorse
For all the ripples on the water
That cast along the foam to slaughter
What makes of life just sad abuse
No, not courageous, just obtuse
I trust myself with loving hue
And, balance all against the few
If none done wrong, I'll never rue
I stroll along the sandy coast
While time stands still and plays the host
To all those thoughts remembered best
Her love, her scent and all the rest
This tempest of the ransomed past
So finely set, uniquely cast
Through all these tendrilled thoughts of mine
That go so far on back through time
The wondrous ripples of the ages
All attest like endless mages
So many lives of trial and error
Are now complete without the terror
A coast across the water seen
An island there that's always been
A barrier of mist between
That shields the lives both crisp and keen
The driftwood fragments here and there
Are fractured far beyond repair
Those precious moments, glimpse a view
Like blue sea glass, so very few
This gentle day of late November
That brings to life all I remember
The beat of life takes hold once more
I walk away from sandy shore

Whickwithy

Landscaping

Look out upon the landscape of the things that mankind does
Forget the past of pain and hurt and all that mankind was
No need to gnaw a limb away to cast away the chains
But, wash away past suffering with flood of summer rains

The Fury

Like Nietzsche's quote, the teeth can show, to snarl with all the best
It only eats your heart and soul and, then just leaves the rest
A haunted husk, a rotted core, the way in which we cling
It may seem narcissistic, but I'd like to keep that thing
That special feeling that all life is high above the waves
Where all the humans dance and sing for what it is she craves
Embrace the day and feel the wind that's blowing in your face
And, feel the breath and pulse and heart of life with all its grace

Shadows

Deep shadows often come my way
But, never do they come to stay
Night shadows from the tree speak of a distant, haunting fear
The darkness all around will make it seem so very clear
Speak not to me of distant fear nor will to lie in state
Send the worry on its way, whiplash the lying trait
Beyond the shadows lies the truth
Deep in the heart of sighs and youth
There lies the bold and windswept ways
Of shining sun and golden bays
Yes, shadows often come my way
But, sunlit helm, no more to say

Ripples too

I skip a stone across the pond and watch the ripples form
And ponder long the way in which my thoughts move past the storm
What wonders of this life exist, as ripples reach the shore
Reflected back, the ripples cross, confusion at the fore
A sigh of depths releases the past, I shake my weary head
Where did the ripples start, reflex, what is it that they bled
A time of life, like parting waves, the trough seems just so deep
But, now, the ripple settles down, and into life I leap
But, no, not yet, a little while, as ripples settle down
A time of peace, a time of thought, the time is coming round

Light and shadow

Turn to face into the light, dark shadow left behind
Gaze into eternity, pure bliss is what I find
The shadow just a mockery of all that's good and kind
Don't let it win the war of wills and creep into your mind
When deep within the shadow's shape, you'll feel that you are blind
With brightest heart, eyes open wide, just let the world rewind
The book will open to the touch, the sounds of life the bind
The beauty bound within each page, the feast of life defined
Now, pause upon the mountaintop, all preciousness refined

~~No Name~~

~~I surely must apologize for being, oh, so bold~~
~~I mostly like to talk of life just as it does unfold~~
~~But, there is something's bothered me~~
~~It's like a line of poverty~~
~~For almost all humanity~~
~~Is fixed into this vanity~~
~~To think of only self~~
~~I watch the interactions and I always see, 'me first'~~
~~No thought of any other, and no loving, dying thirst~~
~~To be so seen from other's eyes as loving, dying noble~~
~~Integrity and honor and one's self-esteem so mobile~~
~~As to pass without a thought~~
~~May I die before I'm brought~~
~~To sit on such a shelf~~
~~Excuse me, then and, if you please, for this sporadic mumble~~
~~But when it is I cough up phlegm, I often tend to rumble~~

The wilderland

Once upon, in farthest time, the world was cold and dark
Built on such a wilderland to break the strongest heart
Tempest raged against the thought that life could be so stark
Then, one day, a glimmer came, cascading joy to start
For as the sun rose o'er the land
The wild fell down and life did stand
Upon a land both bright and fell
Tomorrow came, whose heart can tell

Where away?

Where away, my gentle one? Where is it that you go?
Remember on your journey far one thing that you should know
This life can wear away those things that matter most of all
For if you are not careful, by the wayside they will fall
These precious things that are so rare, but so define a life
Can grind away beneath the stones of time and stress and strife
Of Honor, Soul, and Dignity, important things they be
Respect for all, disdain for none; with Heart, Integrity
And, Love, let's not forget the one that makes it all worthwhile
Such fragile, precious gems, they are, that wear away with guile

Patience

Have you ever seen sun's shadow move
A moment's patience so
Or watch the tide swing, just to prove
It moves from high to low
A little longer patience that
A large part of the day
To watch the seasons pass the hat
Is, yet, a longer way
But, watch a life just pass on by
No heart to leap, nor will to try
No, patience can but watch and cry

Destiny

Destiny
Can set you free
If you understand
On through the maze
The Heart unfazed
If you know the plan
There is no single beat to it
No chance one size fits all
But if you keep your feet to it
The dance will heed the call
Don't stumble on through misery
Nor dazzle to the wizardry
There is no hook into your gills
Nor beacon high upon the hills
But as you glide along the street
Or gaze or blink along so fleet
Set in a moment all its own
A seed will burst through fully grown
And if that seed is fair and fine
'Tis not the mundane nor malign
You feel it in your deepest heart
Your soul can feel it from the start
Beyond the plodding sorely done
Upon that day beneath the sun
You pause and take a little break
A brighter way for you to make
And like a disappearing act
You disappear and come right back

The first day of your life

It's often said to lead your life as if this were your last
Sometimes, I think it's best to live as if there were no past
There comes a time of weight of depths on shoulders that have dared
A shrug upon that weight can save the heart that always cared

The heart of fire

Let's take a step along the way and walk into the heart of fire
What beauty do you see as all the flames of life transpire
So, did you grub along in life, utility a must
Or, did you throw heart open wide to revel life in trust
This life is so much more than rocks and dirt and railroad ties
All chance of beauty some will lose because they analyze
To try to measure life, the beauty's lost before you start
Where did you lose the fire that's built so deep within your heart
There's magic in this life so deep, of that you can be sure
Deeply hidden in between the tears and sighs so pure
Vibrations of a string are just the noise of sounding wave
But, waves of life are music, as you step into the stave
Breathless sights surround you, now, and always with each step
The hidden patterns in the air and flame the wind has kept

Picturesque

There have been times within my life that seemed so picturesque
That left in mind an imprint of a complex arabesque
A feel, a smell and pattern left across the fields of mind
All senses are arrayed to swell the heart and later find
A vision, blinding, in its gift to take the breath away
Triggered by a sight or scent or song I seldom play
A song in heart that sings a sigh that only my heart hears
A surge of soul that slumbered deep across the spanning years
Perchance to waken at the slightest hint of something past
That thunders through the senses with full weight and fully massed
Eternal sighs, again, might be a phrase that I could use
But, breathless, from the memory, the word that I would choose
All beauty binds a way of life that captures as it sends
It happens just so often now, I wonder what portends
A hint of things to come? Of pure beauty's final race?
I staggerdrop and wonderfall at thought I might embrace
That all of life completes the dream, reflected in a face

The titan struggle

The titan struggle of them all is not as it may seem
It comes to one along the way in regal, verdant dream
Impatience is emboldened with the path that's here and now
Eternity, the loss is writ, along the wind somehow
Then, describe the wall that hangs upon the endless frame
When all that all the crowded see is flashing thoughts of fame
The creeping and the facile face reflect not in the glass
Nor cross within the fastness of the catacombs we pass
'Tis not upon the way, these ways, that realms, so far, are lost
The Shooting stars and nebula are like a smoking cross
They pass along within you, now, but never will take hold
The depths and strengths of will that make much more than what is told
It's weighed upon with endless time, the whirlwind holds you down
Must wrestle with a titan strength to win the endless crown
The raves of sadness passing by as waves upon the ear
Like falling through a wisp of air, you guide without the fear
The guidance, like a warm and gentle hand, in which you snug
Life begets the life and love and heart with which to hug
The many faces of the titan struggle flay the small
Whence the will is on the way, the traveler will stand tall
Wary of the wolf and lamb, he stands upon a cliff
With strength of tides and crashing waves, the endless, boundless rift
No more, this life, the fell, dire wolves will ever make a stand
No more the creeping through the golden forest of the land
It pounds upon the shore's steep rocks
In waves of strength to open lochs
Sweeping fast along the way and through your world like fire
Bursting through the broken dreams in waves that never tire
Changing all along the way with wash of love for all
Once again, it will be seen, the traveler standing tall

The Impossible Day

Every day when I wake up
Put something bold into my cup
A fancy smile or something fey
A thought to last throughout the day
And, if a little silly too
A smile could last the whole day through
I see, a few examples, now
Might help the what, but not the how
If speed of light were tied unto
The rate at which the cosmos blew
What, then, would happen, if the fact
Expansion went and jumped the track?
Your dog, like mine, might be quite sweet
But, what if he began to tweet?
This all may seem quite silly
But surely is the point
Like wobbly, new born filly
Would, so surely, day, anoint
A special feeling for the day
To keep the oft-mundane at bay
One of my favorites of all time
My baby's birthday danced in rhyme
And one she'll never understand
To watch the sun rise o'er the land

Petals

Bright petals of the day are strewn across our winding path
So, step and pick them up, just once, and smell the season's laugh
And, as I wander through this life, I pick the petals more
For there, alone, is where the life is on the path to soar

The growing day

From time of dark, before the light
Until that time day triumphs night
I sit within my woods and watch
The glory grow in sylvan notch
I take the time to watch in wonder
As daylight builds the world asunder
The signs of day are slowly coming
As subtle as a thrush's thrumming
No doubt can be, you'll watch too long
For lovely as a thrush's song
As first momentous glimpse of light
That tolls the end of blackest night
With vaguest glance, the world is etched
No depth, no tint, just briefly sketched
And, then, the slightest silver slips
Upon the world to touch the tips
And sharpened edges come to fore
But still in gray from star to core
So slowly, all along the depth
The thief along the border crept
To steal away night's deepest black
He enters through a narrow crack
Behold, for now, the day will start
And coal and char will now depart
It is beginning of events
That lead to wondrous day, immense
I tremble, now, as night relents
But, sun has yet to cross the fence
Yet, now the world begins to form
In shades of gray, no colors warm
Still, whether it is spring or fall
No way the eye can tell at all
There's still no color to the leaves
As, night to day, does slowly ease
And, then, a hint, the softest brush
The barest tint comes with a rush
Now lanes of light pass through the trees

Whickwithy

Untouched, it taps me on the knees
As welcome as a morning breeze
True morning's here, at last, to seize

Innocence

A flock of feelings far above
On wings of hope and heart and love
The sighing winds give lift and blow
And bring to me the afterglow
Of wonder and of fate
So sing to me, sweet shaded grove
Of green and blue, this treasure trove
The waves of life sing to the shore
This land of love bring to the fore
Please, never to come late

Life's cornucopia

Life, it rattles round and round
So many parts we play
Always magic, sight on sound
We must arrange the way
The cornucopia we fill
We've done it all, we say
Filled the horn, headlined the bill
How to make it through this time
How interesting today
Ah, the magic in the rhyme
Is how I wend the way
The magic of a loving friend
Will keep the wolves at bay
And, the love we boldly send
Can shoot a blinding ray

The End

Whenever it happens, whatever the will
I am surely steady
Shaky to think, but I say it with thrill
I think that I am ready
Whether heaven, or nothing, or come back, again
It does not really matter
Or a different eternity, planet or zen
I will not fight the clatter
I am ready, right now, for what is in store
With a snarl and a smile
I'll shake it off now and come back for more
I cannot, now, defile
If this is it, the ignominious end
I catch a silent tear
But, what the heck, there's naught to fend!
There's nothing left to fear
No pun intended there, but with this case, the end
There's nothing there so dear
A ins this life complex, in which we now do wend
The way is never clear
And, if it is to heaven, for hell I feareth not
Then what is it, to wit
It seems, it must be, sure, a certain boring spot
That wings should then be fit
But, if, as I believe, there's life much further on
Then, surely, I rejoice
The rhythm and the dance will carry us along
The song is in my voice
Together
Forever
Just for this case
I now will brace
Am ready to face
That last final grace
In which we all chase
The end

Whickwithy

Springtime

The murmurings of spring attend the world tonight
Such breathless feelings sing of wild heart and delight
The white has turned to green and red
Snow's gone without a trace
The flowers burst up in their bed
Life quickens to the pace

All heart

Strip away facade' and all you find is heart
No will to conquer world, no lofty goal to start
A phantom reverie of soil with little sod
All heart is what I am, when you strip away facade
?

Shining bright

The lands that lie beneath the sun
So softly brushed and gently done
The fields of heart that revel more
The mountains thrust the song to fore
And, on each ocean's endless wave
There moves through life, a single stave

Golden sounds

To hear the children's easy laughter
Or, silence of the night
Should hold the will for ever after
With strength for all that's right
Allay the crippled thoughts of man
And bring him here to see
The ways to learn, un-crippled stand
At last, so boldly free

The concrete and the wind

In serendipity I lay
Throughout eternity's long day
To trust the guide that's never seen
As if all life stood in between
The concrete and the wind
All life goes on its wearied way
The wind blows through the depths to sway
And concrete found upon the scene
That acts as if it's never been
But close the window and the blind
Look deep between and you will find
The tender wisp that's never seen
That holds the strength on which I lean
More mighty than the soaring trees
Or quantum vacuum energy
Or all of time's eternity

Chocolate truffe

Whistle with the will of one
Sing a song of soaring sun
Traipse a track of triple tries
Sing a song of soaring sighs
The day is sweet, a chocolate truffe
That's filled with dreams, this life enough

Birds

Some birds, it seems, work very hard to get to where they go
A sweep of wings is what's required if wishing to move fro
Yet, others seldom stroke the air but on the wind they soar
Ahhh, the magic of those wings and wind I do adore

Silly boy

So many things that fascinate
Those strings and trails and those out straight
A detailed study is required
Of things of which I've never tired
Such fascination in relation to the whims of time
And how it is that I could be so clearly on the dime
I revel in all things I do from dawn unto the dusk
A wave, a rock, such simple things, no, life's no empty husk
Sometimes I feel a silly boy, this way in which I do
Don't get me wrong, I'm rather proud of having held so true
Through time and heart and corporate bowel
An, never throwing in the towel
At fascinating life

The ocean's waves

The ocean's waves do bring a peace
'Til all heart's problems seem to cease
The feelings of contentment are so soft and, yet, profound
The love of all, connectedness, is there within the sound

whippoorwill

The whippoorwill to brighten day
Sings his song as if to say
Good morning to the flower, to the sun, and to the sky
Today is meant for frolicking, so on the wing I fly!

Footsteps in the snow

It may happen that you find deep footsteps in the snow
But, surely, this need never mean you'll not your own way go
Don't follow footsteps in the snow simply because they're there
Just think of where it is you go and take what steps you dare
Then, think about it, once again, and take those steps with care

The wind

I listened to the wind while on its way
It whispered through the trees as if to say
The whirlwind's coming, as it always does
All things will change, with nothing as it was
That is all life, that is what comes with time
All ages pass, 'tis not the chaos mime
The signal breeze is all that you will feel
As sighing trees surround you when you kneel
Partake of love, partake of life and will
For, through it all, the wind will be there still

The Last Bastion

When all is lost, there's nothing left, the war is at the door
Why is it that you'll battle on, what brings you back for more?
Is fame or money or power or pride the price that is to be?
To flicker on and shoot upright, to keep the flame, not flee?
Where is the armour shielding all, the will to face the fates?
Where is the strength to never fall? like mothered pearl the plates
How do you keep the honor true while fighting subtle wars?
No will to die when all is lost while in those corridors
For only this can make it all so clearly worth the while
To struggle on through darkest age, to take each step with style

Freedom

There comes a time in all our lives when it will surely be
That one will look around the world and one will clearly see
The sun arising in the east, the bird, the squirrel, the bee
And, he will know, forever more, that this was meant to be
There comes a time in all our lives, when it is meant to be
That one will look around their life and they will surely see
The wind upon the water and the sail upon the sea
And, one will know, forever more, that he is purely free

Whickwithy

Do you understand?

The way the heart can always last
And bring the sweetness from the past
It's wonderful to say it's true
That bittersweet shall never rue
For life is all and nothing more
Can waken from the heavy score
That this belief is all it takes
To cure the fate or will that aches
The power of this thread is so
Release the hand and let it go

Think again

And, if that thought you thought today conflicts with all you knew
Will you open up the book, embrace a newborn view?
Homesteads arrayed all sparkling neat
Fragmented mountains, country seat
Tempest oceans swing to beat
And all of this for you

The bard

The pain of life might seem quite hard
But, with no pain, there is no bard
The bitter and the sweet combine to make a sturdy soul
Takes storms and sunny days to mark and make a world a whole

The Iron Will

Make of this an Iron Will
No bend, no break, with diamond drill
The eyes, they laser to the sight
Through all the froth, onto what's right
The Iron jaw chews brittle glass
And makes of pain a thing of past

Blossoms

Plant the seed in fertile soil
Into new life it bursts
Yes, indeed, there's time for toil
You'll never quench that thirst
A blossom grows, new life, again
And so begins the tale
For each new blossom is a friend
Both hearty and so hale
A blossom here, brings blossoms there
And, on and on it goes
No need, no chance to capture care
And, once again, it shows
That life, and love, and lessons learned
Are all so much the same
That, with it all, it must be earned
And, never can be tamed

Fantasies and Joy

Life should be a celebration, joy throughout the day
Yes, I live in fantasy and, yes, that is my way
To waste my time on melancholy seems embrace of gloom
So, if I am to build this life and follow my own doom
There is no need for landmines, if so lightly I do step
The flowers brush against my skin, the joy within is kept
I'll never bow my head down low, for anger or in thrall
To say that I have never wept would, simply, not say all
The pain inside a human can be swept away in time
But, only if the pain is seen as broken lines of rhyme
Believe that joy's contagious but, then, so is aching heart
It's all in the perception taken with you from the start
How much the pain can be contained and finally overcome
Before the beating ends the day with final beat of drum
But, one must gaze on up the road for just a little ways
So, one can find the time to sprinkle joy on many quays

Whickwithy

Best of both worlds

Minds of light and stirring thought
Waves of life and all that's wrought
Ripples cross from there and back
Never lost along the track
Just let the ripples amplify
And bring, once more, eternal sigh

Stirrings

The stirrings of its newness that did tremble at the touch
The breath of life and heart and soul did promise, oh, so much
In fear that I would shake its form with slightest gaze or thought
I settled by its newness, so, to bide with what it sought
The stars they brightened and the universe came more alive
Creation's sigh, so wondrous, that built bridge from which to strive
Serendipity had found the link
And, sleepless nights gave one to think
Of slightest stirrings growing strong
And, how they'll live forever long
Transforming all that eye does see
And mind does think and heart decree
I paint with words, she speaks with eye
And stirrings grow, once more, less shy
And, now, the form of life will stand
And ripple slowly 'cross the land
The stirrings are complete

The forest and the trees

If I shout and no one hears, am I really free
Hide behind the forest's depth or hide behind a tree
The wicked ways of willingness does wander with the breeze
If brushed aside, the ghost of time does brush away the trees
But, still the forest, sturdy, stands across this length of land
To tick away the meaning of the time within the sand
Spread forth your leaves, so brindle bright
And, find the meaning in the sight
For you, alone, will see

Ripples

The stirrings have all settled, now, with ripples far and wide
The ripples now advance the thought with slow and steady stride
When all the people of the world reach out to find the best
And, each one in their signal way, will find their way is blest
The ponds, the rivers, trees and stars with passion passed between
That lay upon this world, just now, that vision oft unseen
It lies there for the steps to take, but takes no will at all
Just add the thought that all is right within this hallowed hall
Transcendent thoughts beyond this realm will reach the final day
And, we will hold the sally forth, for now, no longer fey
We stride now far beyond this world, we ride upon the wave
Just, once more, slightest stirrings of the thought we always crave

Waves

The ripples have become the waves that pass from shore to shore
Wave on wave of joy is sent and, then, of course, s'more
There is no end in sight for final wave of joy to be
But, cresting now is tidal wave of joy for all to see
I dive in deep below the waves of life and joy that's sought
The splash of heart is sparkling, now, in crest of loving thought
On beyond the coast of time, beyond the swirling pool
Of the past and drudgery, before the time that you'll
Become much more than painted wall
As all alive await the call
And time stands still to grace the hall
And leaves us whole, to wit

Confidence and doubt

Confidence and doubt, what a struggle it can be
To thunder up the mountainside, complete the glory we
Began upon the open plain, where eye can see the bend
Of world that slopes away on skids, no weapons left to fend
The sting of arrows flung at you from depths of your own mind
Strip bear the thought and ponder deep, just waiting to unwind
It must be crazy, half insane, to think that you can do
Take a sigh and say, again, I can if I wish to

Whickwithy

Petals 2

I brush the petal on the cheek and feel as if I live
The colors of the petals sing, once more, for me to give
It takes the touch of other soul
To make of life much more than dull
To bring to life the petals with the world and thoughts of mine
The majesty of wondrous souls, makes life so very fine
I celebrate today the souls of all that give and care
I relish in the wake of all adventures that I dare
Throw out, once more, arms open wide
With steady thoughts and steady stride
My heart, once more, it sighs

Despair

Go shadow away, don't you darken my door
With pomp and with gloss, I will treat you no more
A tribute to some who would think not to care
No tribute of mine laid, at all, for despair
The trip of the tongue wants to lash out in woe
At spiders and flies and at worlds we don't know
To pass all the time, wait, impending the doom
Just flick it away, and, for heart, make more room
To stand in the doom, wander on with the sparks
To bequeath to the gloom all the wonder of larks
To flutter through time, with the will and the wind
Remember, my friend, to the dream, always pinne

Elopement

Scattered among the broken dreams of daylight past
Find within yourself the tempo strong and fast
Dreams are endless, replenished strands of hope
Wayward ties, beneath the pulse elope

Play to the passion

To the point where passion plays
The fear is always that it flays
Or, that it's here but never stays
Just passes through the endless maze
The sighs are deep
The heart will keep
The song of life for one
Embrace the tune
Shun not the swoon
Shine on just like the sun
The joy of singing, keys, and frets
The boldness far beyond what lets
A triple try is all it gets
Like loving kiss, the lip it wets
And on and on it goes

Mirrors, again

As the tide does wash away the feelings that have come
I find the heart will, once again, take tally of the sum
Each mirror reflects differently, the person that I be
The chains that hold the mirror fixed, will never let me free
Just walk, away
Is what I say
Broke image, there no more
Is that really me I see
No need to go explore
Reflected in the life of me
In some sense, final door
To open wide and walk on through
Dress, once again, in style
Brush the past from coat of blue
And, walk on through with smile

The universe and all

To study all the universe from single grain of sand
A speck of dust, no more than life, to force my willing hand
To revel in the mastering of single, slightest deed
It breaks apart like crystal shards, the shattered soul is freed
Attend the way in which we love and savor sweetest heart
Transform the universe in song with willingness to start
A new, a bold, a wicked step, this heart does surely plead
To salvage off the shatterfall and never let her bleed
I'd lief explore the universe through single beating heart
The sand is not the same as heart, for beat, it plays a part
The sand is glitter in my eyes, I see so clearly how
Sparkle kisses, funniness, the heart is here and now
Funny how those living things popped right before my eyes
Once gone, all there, a magic trick, performed with pure surmise
One day, an antiseptic world, so clean, no life could smirch
Next day, a walk into the woods, as if attending church
The singing and the humming, now, surround me on my walks
The heart uplifts, the life it grows, the universe it talks

Beyond the wind

For somewhere past the final glance, where concrete thought can't reach
There lies a quick and agile trance, no will can ever teach
Like sparks of fire, so uncontained from deepest heart of sun
All life bursts free, all joy explodes, no debtors ever dun
The twilight speaks unto this pulse and screams its right to be
All waking thought, in shock and awe, stands stuttering with glee
The jet of stars
The stars jet by
In blink of eye
The world stands still
To watch it fly
The heart will fill
With satin sigh
A breath is lost unto the wind
All thoughts cascade and sighs rescind

Whickwithy

The sea

The ripples build as in a trance
Transformed to waves across expanse
And both do mask the swell
Far beneath the surge is strong
Massive movement deep and long
What strength, we cannot tell
And, then the tide adds its effect
A massive touch of moon's respect
Transcend, we will not quell
From crest, we see the daunting sky
From trough, the sea will capture eye
And, sudden, feel so fell
Conditions perfect for the merge
With ripples, waves, and swelling surge
Surf's rocket does propel

Open Wide

I spread my arms out opened wide, lean back, I fall into
The open arms of life that hold me close and pass me through
To open, warm and gentle arms of loving in this life
No need, I find, to cringe away, facades are all the strife
Like stepping stones upon a pond, that stand above the wave
And save me from a drowning end, life's arms are all I crave
All nature brings me closer to the feel for such a way
It's never far from nature will you ever see me stray
But, nature, all alone, can only be there for so much
Above the waves, upon the stones, one craves the human touch

A broken way

Of grace and honour, balance true
I bow down in such a state
Unlike the scalloped, armoured few
The churl has no such fate
He will swing his blithered gaze
To all the pomp and glitter
Sad ending to his fractious praise
Transformed to twisted bitter
To trudge along
No heart, no song
The sighing cry
So late the sky
And end the life no fitter

The wandering ways

It's sad to say about our ways
That malice is so strong
The heart it plays but, then, it strays
From life within the song
How does it happen
Don't ask me
I haven't got a clue
The lips are flappin'
Thoughts won't be
Of honor, heart, and true
When dragged on through the mire
It seems to just inspire
A loss of honor, life and soul
So much to lose, to gain, be whole
Must strengthen heart and battle through
This war, don't lose, for it is you
Embrace eternally the list
Of lives you've spent in mornings blissed
To gain, again, the heart, so dear
To wipe away that shedded tear

A way forward

It's sad to say about our ways
That malice is so strong
The heart it plays but, then, it strays
From life within the song
To gain the heart and move the beat
To reign upon the mountain's seat
And see the misted fall
For one must raise their troubled gaze
Look, once upon the world unfazed
And strain into the all
No end in sight
No troubled fright
Will ever match the will
When step is light
The distance right
No way in which to fill
For time it has no end
The endless way will wend
Once more, unbend, "Stand tall"

Delusions of grandeur

Some might say my delusions are so grand
But, not for me, for all of life and land
Just brace you heart, make bold the soul
If I'd one wish, they'd both be whole
Delusion far exceeds the waste
This day eternity you'll taste
And quit this spin on merry-round
For once your soul is finally found
That soul, once lost, is safe and sound

The way forward

As you know, my precious one
I've never been that much of one
To follow blindly those that lead
And, those that spout a crippled creed
Each day the more I am convinced
And, so, the more do I evince
That life's pursuit is one true love
There's nothing else can touch thereof
We must complete the final trip
For which we are so well equipped
Because we settle for the rain
We come back time and time, again
And, never to move on in essence
For only in your finest presence
The final call just cannot be
Unless a lifetime's spent with thee
What of god that I could need?
But, love of you completes the deed
When just one life's been spent together
A new, sweet bliss will hold the tether
Then, on to new and brighter shore
Beyond the sound of waves that roar

Poetry

Poetry is not a poet's tool
To separate the wisest from the fool
Nor, is it that a poem is complete
Unless the words and rhyming are replete
Complexity may satisfy the authors
The reader only wonders why he bothers
To paint a scene or world in only words
To whisk away the heart on wings of birds
This is the task and challenge of the poet
So sad there are so few that truly know it

The Travelers

Once the day was folded up and, then, been put away
The travelers toasted final cup 'fore ambling on their way
The weary Dream donned raincoat pale, the darkened road to face
Staid Principles' so well-worn cloak was slowly shrugged in place
They trudged along together then, at quite a lonely pace
Both broken rhyme and deepest ruts were oft the dismal case
Along the darkened road there stood gloom's shadows here and there
The massive mound of rocks looked vaguely like a well-worn care
A tree of disappointment seemed like end of all that's known
They slowly moved together as they heard a ticking moan
But, what was that they saw ahead, a traveler on the road
They brightened just a little, then, for good he seemed to bode
Ah, bright Heart, in tattered tails, you comfort all you see
The aching back of Principles from bitter drudgery
And saddened eyes of tired Dreams that sheltered from the art
Did lose their pain, forevermore, in presence of great Heart

Serendipity's plan

Broken pieces lightly tossed
Some are found and some are lost
No crippled creed allowed to bear
The slightest fruit, the slightest stare
The warrior's spirit must be shattered
The pieces all, already scattered
Now build it, once again, from scratch
New mind, new heart, and will to match
The warrior spirit recognize
Through steady gait and solemn eyes
And, now, my warrior, you I boast
You'll battle back and make the most
But, battleground has changed
All signposts rearranged
The tides will stop
The moon will crop
You bend time to your will

Whickwithy

The Traveler

The Dreams, and Heart, and Principles are in the Traveler
He fended off the worst of fates, and broke Unraveler
Ignored the bounty on his head
Poured purest love, Great Heart's one med
To highest peak, the Dreams were led
And, Principles not put to bed
And, on through life he goes
Sometimes, he travels past the mark, he'll pause to just unwind
His back against a tree, he leans, for there, he'll surely find
Such curios as never seen
Of life and love held in between
He'll pick them up, so much to glean
Just brush them off and make them clean
He grasps bouquet and throws
The smile is on his face, once more, for memories long past
He steps along to trace the route, to hold his love at last
A thoughtful pace is led this way, his hands behind his back
With pensive brow and eyes to ground, perceives just what he lacked
Wider steps, and quickened pace, he steps from star to star
And, reaches up, grasps cosmic rose, with widest steps, so far
For, now, his pace, beyond the realm, with galaxies beneath
Is out the end of universe, his steps will now bequeath
He bows down low, presents to her, a cosmos all her own
For she is all to heart and soul; true love, the gift she's shown

Three travelers

Three travelers, trudged further on, to keep appointments made
Staid Principles stood 'gainst a world of slow, relentless fade
The Dreams to build all future lives much better than the past
Great Heart to hold the core that makes a life like this so vast
Ahead, a storm's about to brew, of drudge and lonesome times
But, Dreams just opens cloak of hope to shelter three in rhymes
From worst monsoon their world has seen, the worst of times yet gone
In this, the Principles and Heart were played, as if a pawn
But, shelter from the winds and rain provided by the Dreams
Their world will hold together, now, at least, that's how it seems
The storm of life does slowly pass and further on they go
To mountains high and rugged pass on which they move so slow
But Principles' harangues and shouts, "with love, this also ends
With sturdy strength, and laser eyes, and, most of all, our friends"
And, steady on, the mountain's peak is bent to will's full strength
Of Principles, held in reserve, along the breadth and length
Of vistas that take breath away with wonder and with light
Once more, they know the path is clear and all is, once more, right
So, now, the three continue on, and now, approach the shore
Vast ocean spans horizons wide, they pause in thought, once more
Staid Principles is staggered down by how to pass this halt
And, Dreams looks on and sighs so deep, it seems like endless fault
Great Heart just smiles and wraps the two in wonderful embrace
"You see, my friends, we're finally there, await the final grace"
And, from the sea, she rises up, like water-born esprit
She smiles a smile from watered eyes that, lastly, they can see
For tears have washed away all pain and sighs, the four, let out
And, from the Heart the sigh is turned into the greatest shout
For all the pain and suffering of all the lives' long care
Has brought eternal love back home to meld the loving pair
Eternity's own open door, they finally look out
Upon the vast array of love, they gaze without a doubt
All shadows pass, the Heart is whole, the favored Dreams come true
And, Principles can take a pause to take the time to view
The love of Heart so very strong and built to last all time
And sing a song of true romance, and dance the love in rhyme

Whickwithy

Ricochets of the heart

As waves of this life rush on over me
The tides of the times will now set me free
And give of the heart that one reason to go
As on we progress just so soft and so slow
The tempest of life always plays its own part
In the wild, unrestrained ricochets of the heart
That message of hope that was cryptically sent
So glowing with heart and so clear with intent
The rainbow of colors that felt so profound
Like a flicker of light and the surf as it pounds
A wave of your hand and a thousand hearts flutter
The heart rocks, once more, as volcano would shudder
The heart has been caught, a full trip, sudden stutter
And, then it begins with that rumble and mutter
Of well-tested times and the whirlwind of days
Of shallowest shores and an ocean that plays
As I turn and I look, in flies a new dart
I stumble to knees, ricochet of the heart
The wonder is there, that I never will doubt
The pages of script I will just do without
For etched in the heart from those lives and all times
Are scribed with the deepest, fundamental of rhymes
The trip-hammered heart, not a single bit less
And, passion for life will go on, I confess
I arch to the sky with the wind through my hair
Arms out open wide, I embrace all I care
A tremble is there, I have felt from the start
Whenever there flies ricochets of the heart
I'll shout down the heavens that dare disagree
For there, in the heart, is where I shall be
Just frolic and dance, all the pain will depart
As I feel, just once more, ricochets of the heart
No tepid warm heart is this fierce heart of mine
It flares and it burns, and so brightly does shine
To while away hours, at piddle and chore
Not while the notes sing, far away, to the score
Within such a life, I stand calmly apart
And catch, just once more, ricochets of the heart

Whickwithy

Seasons

October 1, 2008, Pine Point, Maine

Now, at last, I have the time
To celebrate these loves of mine
The waves of life wash over me
To cleanse the soul and set me free
I spend my time in awe and wonder
Cast adrift but not asunder
I see you bright in my mind's eye
It's sealed so tight with every sigh
No trouble to recall your face
Those freckles fixed in time and place
We soar the night, the hearts beat soon
We dream the light and sing the tune
No rushing now, no frantic mess
And, now, at last, I feel so blest
And, now I also celebrate true Nature and her glory
The seasons sing their daily fate and craft their yearly story
The leaves are in a wonder time, but soon they will be gone
All lost once more beneath the rime, once more just winter's pawn
An odd time it does surely seem to restart such a life
As winter's hoary frost begins to cut like Nature's knife
But, always, always I believe in Serendipity
So now must be the perfect time to let my life go free
For as we dance the whirling dance and sing the song in tune
We traipse the brightest pattern, yet, beneath the summer moon
Just wait and we will see the steps of bursting life in June
And see if I have wrought the dance to seal the silent boon
It seems to me this verse should last, at least, a year to date
The seasons will have, then, all gone, this poem's met its mate
A little random wandering should surely be its fate
For wand'ring, oh, so very long, I surely hold this trait
I wander in the thought, and so, it wanders in the beat
As if I wondered at the dance that makes this life a treat
A song just danced on through my mind, an anchor I should be
While it is sure and, oh, so true, my mate so anchors me

Whickwithy

We anchor far beyond this day, right through the heart of time
For it is through eternity, this endless love we climb
My love, my dear, my darling one, you know it's all for you
The winds of life can never throw us from the bold and true
So, it may be twin anchors there beneath the bow and stern
The cross-winds clear and tantamount to what we have to learn
The cold and dreary rains of autumn have, just now, appeared
To wash away all color and to leave the grey so clear
This grey all by its lonely self, a season of the year
The grey and calm before the white, I do not shed a tear
A good and reminiscent time to think of you, my dear
Look out upon the rain today, upon the leaves that fall
There's so much here to savor, now, for here is autumn's call
I don't regret the change of life to start in autumn days
For it was time to start to live and practice new found ways
To rein the heart was first mistake, so many years ago
But not this time, free rein it has, so it can find the flow
The heart does pulse the pale and pride
The seasons set so sure
And when I have ignored this guide
The heart was still the cure
I left behind a wilderness of corporate conundrum
There was no sign of light finesse, just nothing but the numb
I now explore a wilderness of wild heart and delight
Resplendently unfolding in a life that will ignite
The wondrous ways of Life's hid not, nor are they on display
Like love that we so often seek, the art is in the play
Tremendous when unhidden, slow, but just beyond the sight
The bold, the brave, the bidden flow, the path is not the plight
Beyond the daily drumming, far beyond the dulling pall
Beneath the hoary rime and mundane-ness of it all
The glory shines, forevermore, for all, intense and strong
A simple joy is always there, a thrill to last lifelong
That pulse is from the heart's strong beat, it will not be denied
To let it beat its measure and to glimpse the joy un-spied
A glowing, loving treasure, in this life, beyond the ride
To look, just now, and there it lies, full well the loves betide
A life that's now worth living or a life that does confide
The joy of being living and the joy of life not lied

That awesome autumn has moved on and fallen by the way
To pass along to ages gone and leave the days of gray
So gray are clouds and Nature too
But gray is not the thought I choose
The bright blue skies were painted fuller
Redrawn now with charcoal duller
Somehow, on through this fickled time
That so bestirs the ring and rhyme
Slow silence, deep, descends
And softness all depends
Upon the moment next
As all of life reflects
From past so very distant
No thought of heart resistant
The life goes on persistent
From now unto its end
So many rhymes and many plays
So many lines to pen
For me, it's always new found ways
Their love, two ladies send
My Lady Love just shines so bright
My Lady Nature in her might
They make my fondest days
The bitter and the cold onrushing, paint the falling night
The crisp, clean air and stars still shine for me forever bright
The place of fire is working now to stave off all the cold
And turkey from Thanksgiving now is just a few days old
The rambling nature of these days
So matches well this poem's plays
That wander on from here to there
Without the slightest bit of care
I chop the wood to burn the fire
The days so short, they never tire
But nights are long and weigh the deeps
The time to dawn just slowly creeps
But, still the grey time holds the sway
And, soon, we'll see bright winter day
A whisper, yet, the time will be
As snow descends to set fall free

Whickwithy

I toss the logs and hear the hiss
Of sun and ice and living bliss
Today the rain and ice did litter
Crystal trees and diamond glitter
So beautiful, but cruel and bitter
Broken trees, the ones left fitter
The sun is barely talking to the earth these latter days
He seems to shun the world right now, just leaving all in haze
But soon he will relent, with his antipathy all spent
And we will all be bent on a path to summer's scent
These days we must remember that
When cold's beneath the heart and hat
The holidays are finally here
And fill the world with certain cheer
There's lots of snow upon the ground
White Christmas now is clearly sound
The chill must never reach the bone
Must warm the heart and hearth of stone
Cruelest winter is the harshest critic
Of the life and of the new-spawned lyric
"And, that you speak of Love", he boasts
"To live, at all, is fine for most
Survival, you should have some doubt
To pass to Spring is no short route"
The chill of winter to the bone
The brittle days in bitter zone
Don't leave it now to think and moan
We sing the salient, toast the tone
The sun does rise to touch the cheek
Across the land, some warmth does leak
But, just a little, now and then
From one, then on, the heart will send
Your footprints in the snow surround
Your heart prints always glow profound
We offer up the whirlwind sigh
Enough to love, enough to try
For Mother Nature, so profound
Her beauteous ranges, so abound
Within the winter's brutal cold

The storied life that's paused is told
The beauty and brutality combine so well her way
We live on, daily, at her whim and shiver at her sway
At any time on any day
Her final furied might could wray
And, so, like magic, autumn's tones
Have coalesce to white as bones
But, ah, the achings soon arise
To glory springtime's warmer skies
The joy of tossing snow is real
The whitened walls of snow reveal
The need for prism's rainbow border
The white's dispersal's now in order
For, once again, let color reign
The springtime's prism, winter's bane
The seasons change, all life repents
But, now I beg that snow relents!!
Here's a fact that most don't know
Some grass is green beneath the snow
The buds are on the trees since fall
Just waiting for sweet springtime's call
Is she always so prepared?
With passion bold and soul that's bared
Not the slightest, least pretense
The thought is just a feast immense
For all of this eternity
Is so well lived with certainty
That cannot be denied
Though often I have tried
The whiff of spring comes way too early
And leaves the heart all hurly-burly
Frosty February's smile
That leaves a longing for awhile
The ache it leaves within the chest
It leaves one panting for the best
And leaves the soul with little rest
Just tasteless tang of trenchant test
As springtime winks and tempts the tale
The winter seems to never fail

Whickwithy

But, just one day? some warmth would please!
Tomorrow, pray, just for a tease
The warmth internal has to do
To keep me from brightest blue
Though blue, my favorite color is, it surely wears too thin
It's really true, I like it well, but not upon my skin!!!
So, here I pause a little while
Till spring bursts through in splendid style
Of winter there's no more to say
Just smile when gone and well away
The deepest frost is short, in fact
Just seems the longest, slowest tract
As all Life's rhythm beat before
We stretch and pop, the Lion's roar!!!
Here comes the warmth! the life to bring!
That's carried on the back of spring
A little fore, a little back
Slowly move along the track
The ruddy red of buds that bulge
The sweetest whispers do divulge
That now the Spring has come
Do not toy with snowflake's burst
No more the wait to quench the thirst
March rains will drown the sum
For life to burst throughout the world
To think of blooms and pretty girls
Cold depths, no longer numb
To walk the beach once more in time
To swing and bat away the rhyme
The depths of life we'll plumb
To burst with joy, no reason more
Life's meaning here is just to soar
The revel moments come
Sing life and beat the drum
Don't blink the eye or you might miss
Some burst of life, some subtle twist
But, glance to see what signs there are
Still only ruddy red so far
From grey to white to ruddy red

Whickwithy

To paint so bold, need more be said?
The autumn colors have all fled
Replaced so soon at beauty's head
Bright colors, soon, in flower's bed
And, as the air becomes so mellow
Days turn bright with red and yellow
The windows open, curtains gone
To wake to birdsongs at the dawn
The stirring life is everywhere
Just take a moment to prepare
The surge of heart is here and now
No equal in all life somehow
It's like the best of all of love
I'll never lose the meaning of
All life reflected in her heart
Bright springtime's burst, that wondrous start
So, throw the windows open wide
Let all the fresh air come inside
The rains of March come sliding in
The fireplace cozy, suits within
I read a book or mend a screen
I stay inside, stay sight unseen
Those dreary rains are timed so well
I've lost my Lady for a spell
No change of heart for me in sight
Forever, still, with all my might
It's sad to say more lives to be
I offer up this life to see
For is it gone till long, dark sleep
Will she come back from darkened deep
Too soon to tell, too close to home
The devastation, like a tome
More words abound to rake the coal
They deep abide and burn the soul
But, that is all I'll say of sad
I pave the way to future glad
To talk of her, again, so bright
My lovely lady of the light
But still the fire is in its place

Of moist and chill, there's still a trace
The flicker of the flames and thought
A special place and time is wrought
The day's so deep within the fog
Best throw the fire another log
This quiet day, no birdsong sigh
Just hear the seagull's lonely cry
The pace of life beats like a heart
That's racing up to this year's start
How can a heart stay truly blue
While life all round is bursting through
I promised her to celebrate
Yes, even in this broken state
For her existence is the key
For my exuberance to be
I own her not, that's never mattered
I sing to world that's still not tattered
As the wind whips through the trees
This is no light and gentle breeze
That blows right through to hit the bone
And make it feel as cold as stone
And, now, my pace of life does slow
As I move on to this new flow
To play this part so new to me
Of strength and will, so well, we'll see
I'll ripple on through days and years
With porous songs and shedded tears
The strength, and will, and tears to match
When heart will naught but to attach
The spring came through just yesterday, could feel it like a fist
Like checkmate on a chessboard, Spring is now upon the list
Like bells inside a tower ring to all those faithful few
To come and celebrate, right now, for god is in the pew
"For I am here", Spring shouts for all, "let be no slightest doubt!
Winter's gone for sure and good, in disarray and rout!
Some skirmishes are left to fight, a battle here and there
But, for the scarves and knitted hats, give not the slightest care"
The brook now babbles, burbles on, while sparkling in the sun
It voices all the love of spring, it sings of joy and fun

The deepest sigh of all I take to move on with bright care
Though gone, she is, for now, it seems, my love for her I'll wear
It is the brightest badge of all for deep and troubled time
I sing the songs of love and life and carry on with rhyme
For this eternal love of ours, won't end with weather changed
Its strength is such to carry on through any road deranged
The seagull's cry is still so lonely
As if they flew with heartstrings only
The green it deepens every day
The ruddy red goes on its way
The leaves and shade will soon replace
The ruddy red in every trace
And, just one rain is all it took
Bold green, and yellow, babbling brook
The simplest pleasures, all I want
To satisfy without the flaunt
And never leaves the slightest taunt
Nor do I care to somehow daunt
For all there is, she says, "Just be"
And let the mind and life go free
Pomposity is not my way
And, never have I had to play
That game to do what I should do
Just trust in heart, so bold and true
A hard way, surely, that is so
Always hard to ever know
Beguile me, if that pleases you
For, even so, my heart is true
For, when, in fact
You've done the act
The ramifications of the act are there on you, not me
For there and then, you've made your case to, then, no longer be
These days it's hard to find the laughter
I ponder, long, the ever after
It's silly of me, that I know
I do not do it for the show
But, what is there that I should know
If not some sense of afterglow
I walk the path that's so well worn

A simple life, so unadorned
It suits me well, somehow it's true
The parks, and flowers and skies of blue
So, down the wooded path I go
I'm wandering, wondering at the flow
Into the wind, it leans and sways
The white birch shoulders Nature's praise
It always evolves, and never resolves the way in which to grow
Like Mandelbrot spot, a plentiful shot, that is this life, just so
The killing cold is gone, right now, but still so cold at night
Unburied from the depths of covers still just such a fright
For spring, no time for patience, and, to dally, is quite rare
When limbs they sing, the blood it boils, and heart has not a care
Yet, life just patiently moves on from bud to burst to bloom
And leaves and ferns take their sweet time to, once again, resume

Flaunt beauty and desire today
So roused, again, by Nature's play
A woman at her loving best
I swoon with awe, no time for rest
Her sigh was wind around the trees
Embraced was I by gentle breeze
This was a day in which to seize
Love and life to fully please
In her honor, life burst through
From leaves to ferns to birds that flew
Their song so joyous on the wing
Of perfect days of sun they sing
An ache so deep was felt within
If time one took embracing wind
The lives rush by so many days
But not today, for Nature plays
All it takes on days like this
Is just a pause to feel the kiss
Dirt beneath the fingernails
The world beneath my feet
Flower garden never fails
To liven hearts that beat
Steady on the course of days

Whickwithy

Each step you take is next
Focus just on Nature's plays
Of life, no thought perplexed
Each seedling like a tine
The garden grows just fine
Bursting flowers soon to come
Mid songs of birds and bees that hum
Spiders with the webs they weave
With all this life, how can I grieve
And, yet, I can today
One more day, one more step
I know my heart is always kept
Just take the sigh so sadly wept
And, steady on the way
A gentle thing that flower garden
Softens even hearts that harden
Then, at last, it seems to pardon
And, sadness cannot stay
For there, in her own way
Is love of life and play
That squirrel just put on quite a show
The dancing tail puts heart aglow
He prances, making trees a path
And, watching this, can't help but laugh
That heartfelt laugh was needed so
The heart, it heaves both to and fro
I swing it up and keep it there
I speak of life without a care
The song of life so much in tune
And, whither of the afternoon
The birds are calling to the morn
My heart today not fully torn
A day for celebration
Of all of life's creation
For me, this day, there's no hard work
It's just occasion's little perk
I take when I have worked so hard
Like yesterday in woods and yard
At building beauty for to see

Whickwithy

With gardens, walks, and park to be
Ah, such a joy in Nature found
Yes, even when heart's run aground
Enough of that, a will away
A bench is built to come and stay
Summertime will be here soon
The burgeoned life looks on to June
The leaves are bursting, buds are blown
As seasons drive the furrowed plow
We're on to warm and shaded days
There's no more fog or glaring haze
'Tis painted clear, the time has come
To lavish life and love succumb
The roaring lion roaring more
The crashing waves awash the shore
Just shake the sand from feet that leaves
To hear the seagull as he grieves
Now, hear the seagull's lonely cry
Upon the wind, he lets it die
It never will come back, again
But, offered up to minds of men
The staggered days are coming
And, the shock seems to wear off
The hummingbirds are humming
And, the fickled seem to scoff
There's new found way to go the course
Don't leave behind the least remorse
Just let the waves wash over me
And, let the wind 'round to the lee
Ah, as the spike is to the moon
For once again, and all too soon
We watch the rocks and sand combine
Like liquid rays, so much like wine
A cold spell passes, one more time, to end the month of May
'Tis once when cut and once when burnt, wood warms me twice today
'Twas such a wind at will, today, that blew June into dwell
It freshens all of life, this way, its task it has done well
Here comes that sharp and crucial pain
As, life moves on, yes, once again

Whickwithy

Where in this life we've never seen
The heart and soul have never been
To flicker through the day to pass
So soft and sparkly, blue seaglass
But, never mind the waves today
For it has come for me to pay
For loving deep beyond the throne
'Tis not the day in which is known
The never-ending love of all
It's just a day to feel the pall
It's time to move on with this life, of that there is no doubt
The bittersweet is here, for now, but there's no need to pout
My Lady's anger has been quelled
But, timber, also, has been felled
The tears are better than the cold
For in this life, be better bold
I say it, once again, to fend
That time will be here in the end
I wait without the slightest thought
Never will I be distraught
While waiting for my Lady
Whenever she is ready
I will be here on through it all
I flicker at the season's call
New growth is all around, right now
It bursts out bold and bright, somehow
So new to life, they just begin
The little squirrels with tails so thin
The fresh new leaves and tender sprouts
All burst with life without the doubts
That trouble me from whence to gone
At least my soul is back from pawn
Two weeks of all that fog and cold, I feel as in a cloister
I finally built a roaring fire, for air could not be moister
'Tis something special when a fire is built within July
A roaring fireplace in the house and, yet, I still don't fry!
It's funny how each day reflects this life's pure joy and pain
This year is so reflected in the long, torrential rain
The scattered tales from winds that swept

No day for loosened feelings kept
'Tis something there within the mud
Besides the careful waxing bud
The paths are clear, the final say
Has kept the fog and cold at bay
And something more in that impression
That casts this summer of confession
It's now, full on, we feel the worst
And, pass along the final burst
The paths will lead us back to right
And, on to day and back from night
The fog has lifted, cold is gone
It feels like life is back for dawn
To shed the demons is the chore
I've shed a few, but there are more
Must make some sense of all of this
And, all that lies within the kiss
One demon is the wrenching change I've forced myself to make
From cozy, comfy, mundane dead to living life at stake
It sounds so easy, sounds so nice
But how is it to go
To learn to live, this once, for thrice
When never did I know
That life is not for show
No longer plodding sandy beach
The rocky coast has now been reached
Sometimes it seems all passes by so swiftly on this ride
Just sleeping on the beach until you're washed up by the tide
One day the day is full of snow
With heart and hearth and love aglow
Next day, two seasons have gone fast
The heart and hearth and life have passed
Idyllic days of summer
On within this certain state
It's looking like a comer
And, the barbecue won't wait
Ah, the secrets so revealed upon the smoking grill
How to keep the tears at bay and find the long lost thrill
Divining more than was bequest

While moving on to next request
All time is on a shorter string as years are clipped and dried
The inch is daily measure, now, where, once, a yard applied
I feel momentum growing like tsunami in the tide
What is it that will wash ashore, of that I have not spied
The shadow movements in the dark
Alone, I flick and then I spark
Revealed by flame throughout all time
The way in which the thoughts combine
Converging once the season's gone
Like evening shadows on the lawn
It's pointing to the subtle fact
That, now, I've gone and, then, come back
I take a sip of coffee and I watch the starscapes reel
Upon the roof, I lay on back, my soul now made of steel
The rains don't want to end this year
Replacement for a missing tear
So, cry for me, if it's your wish, I'll not cry for myself
I fill the day and fill the heart, fill up the largest delft
Though, really, there's no need for tears
I've never held unreasoned fears
The dappled days do dacker down
If days could wear a single sound
It might be heard a church's bell
Pure, crystal clear, a passioned spell
Or sound of breath, so brief, held in
Without the clatter or the din
Of tumult rallied round the cry
And, still, for all, the head held high
Could be it is idyllic days that broke the demon's back
No jabber, now, of toil and pain, no whip around to crack
'Tis funny, though, idyllic day
There doesn't seem so much to say
They're wonderful, and that's a fact
So full of joy, the day is packed
They're not embattled, worn, or aching
So like a sigh that's in the making
The springtime was so busy
With a thousand ways so dizzy

But, now, a pause that is so right
No harking hills or book of might
The Harlequinade on final day
As demons fade and melt away
The breath of trees, relentlessly, sings of the deeds that mount
The nectar of existence flows to fill the swelling fount
This changeling year has made it, nearly, to the final round
So often stumbling on its way but, often, so profound
And, what a year it's been
One season left to spend
My favorite season of them all
I started out and end with fall
It works out well, so far, except
Somehow my sanity I've kept
But, still, there are three months to go
And, if it's lost, I'll let you know
And just in time for summer's reach
I spend my days upon the beach
'Tis such a lovely time of year
I guess I'm sane and in the clear
Picturesque completes the word
I drink this time a toast
Life is loose, the froth is stirred
The sky can surely boast
Of days so fair and clouds so fine
I drink it in like deep, red wine
I give to it the most
I'm drenched in love, my heart surrounds
With all of life's smells, sights, and sounds
I taste and touch my Lady's love
It's all that's left, sent from above
For in this life, the host
Beyond the meaning of the ways
Where crippled hearts and new-born strays
Arrive upon a broken shore
To heal their hearts and guide the score
Onto a crystal coast
To walk the woods and call them home
To soar the heart and let it roam

The spell of pall completely gone
The spell of life, at last, full on
To flicker days of years gone by
I sought the soft, unending sigh
So finely round and softly caught
Forever more, it has been brought
No time at all for mundane lies
I have the heart and will that tries
I have removed the ghost
And, of this feat, I boast
I make of life the most

Sometimes, you know, I have to laugh
For all there is, life's just a gas
To take a thousand days well spent
With all the thoughts and heart well meant
To die at such a time's just fine
For all those thousand days would shine
I begged my soul to let me live
To take of life but, more, to give
I set out, once, as in a raft
The seasons passed upon the craft
As hammock days have come at last
To crew the time, no missing past
I touch the cool and gentle breeze
A cup of tea and book to please
I sense a few leaves, here and there, that ripple in the breeze
As if some wand'ring soul's out there, alone, among the trees
Or, is there now a pair that dance and chase the wondrous day
A game of tag or hide and seek is surely what they play
The mind does mostly go its way without the slightest care
To wrench it through from transit thought, I often do not dare
As rains, once more, come pouring down (and what a summer this!)
I wish to wrench my mind away to wander through the mist
To peer so far between the trees much farther than I've gone
I hope to reach one day, this way, the God-King's summer lawn
Is a fawn or sidhe king hidden by the trees
If I take just fifty steps will life change by degrees?
Or, will an ocean lay before me when I boldly step

Through that open door ahead which glory often swept
I spend such time on thoughts of awe
For what else soars the soul
The jagged rocks and toughened paw
Are left behind with toll
Those trickled tears in windswept days of summer's sliding feast
No more the cave of swallowed time, and freckled rays, the least
Just like the seasons, as they pass, transforming all it's seen
From moment to the moment, now, what changes have there been
Shocking when it's viewed, at last, from distance far away
No change, at all, can there be seen when looking day to day
So, flicker is a favorite word, but why, I cannot say
So, flicker on and flicker out, it's just along the way
There's something shocking in the word
Describes the things that can't be heard
And, now, I press along the line
To watch the rail from far behind
Transforming all beyond the mist
Once been seen and twice been kissed
To make of it just what you will
Hush a moment and be still
A feast for all beyond the sight
Beneath a dim and flickered light
Slow path it takes along the way
For what to wish, I cannot say
Right around the farthest tree
I must be you, I must be me
No paths are there along the stream
Of trickling heart and rippling dream
But, in the night, you're eyes adjust
And, then, you clear away the dust
You now can see the sparkled shine
Of coupled rays, so unrefined
Were never better days than these
Not when I wrote nor when you please
I shatter far away the scale
And far along, the dim and pale
All time does brush against the feel
Of arms, relentlessly, like steel

No matter what the wind, bar none
To find a way that's seldom done
The thoughts, like gems of blue and green that scatter on the beach
So many there, so very rare, and some beyond the reach
So many more are scattered far
Just take a stroll and there they are
'Tis clear the beach, though, has no end
When will the walk no longer wend
It is for me, a saddened thought
The end of all those gems I caught
A ray expands to spark the Jem
Just like a dream in REM
This is no dream or, what you find
Is that it is the waking kind
In which that ray of pure sunshine
And, all the dreams, are waking fine
And, if you walk along the beach
One rule to make is that you reach
Vacation days in which you've tried
To schedule for the day's low tide
So, summon up your dreams and waves
And, put away those blackened days
I can, most days, right there, be spied
Of course, that is, when it's low tide
Easy peasy, I do quote
Long pants and shirt and writing note
As I walk along the shore
'Tis where I wrote most this rapport
The susurration of the wave
That speaks to me and I do crave
To have a conversation there
Though I'm not sure the waves do care
To hear me babble on through time
Of days and joy and triple rhyme
I might just seem a bit of pain
They'd laugh and say, "He comes again!
Who talks to waves as if he knows
Such joy we have in crashing throes
Who shouts at waves and pumps for joy

Whickwithy

There's something there should love employ"
But, flicker on from day to next
The waves still there, the crash perplexed
I did not show upon that day
They shrug and shake as if to say
"Another one, today is gone
They sure don't last so very long"
So, there's the waves that never nap
Oh, yeah, I near forgot cap
This poem's winding towards the end
But, still, about two months to spend
Describing seasons as they go
And, crazy thoughts, as they do grow
I walk into the closet
Take a rhyme off of the rack
No need for a deposit
There's still more just at the back
No squirrel am I of poetry
The rhyme just always seems to be
Another word that sticks to me
Is 'ripple', I just can't get free
I shake and wipe and even flick
But, durn, the word just seems to stick
I take it off the left hand, on the right hand does it go
And, next then, on the left hand, there is 'flicker', don't you know
, ripple on and flicker too
This time, I hope we're really through
With all those words, sheesh, such a chore
To throw away and find some more!
My heartbeat is united
Looking forward to the time
In which the season's sighted
Into the fall we climb
It's still a little ways away
But, so like favorite book or play
Impatiently, I wait
But, I can still create
The images of rustic ways
Recalling reminiscent days

It seems unkind to summer
To look forward to the fall
But, rain has made it glummer
And, it never did stand tall
But, cool it's been, I can't complain
I've learned to just ignore the rain
Go on with what it is I do
I walk the beach, or mow, or hew
So, family begs you visit and the friends say, "Come on down!"
It's hard as heck, as seasons change, to leave without a frown
There's always something more to do around the old home place
The seeds to bed, the flowers to trim, weeds gone without a traceI shear
and shape the lawn with care
Each contour like a shoulder bare
So like my love, so smooth and fair
I'd better halt it all right there
No, surely, I would not compare
No thought, as such, I'd ever dare
But, treat them both with tender care
And, as I learn the contour
And, the shape and way they grow
The knowledge is just way too poor
The empathy must show
Just trip a heart and what you find
A little love will just remind
Of life in living wonder
And, the sweetness sans the blunder
For time and thought shall come as one
No seasons change without the sun
To stir the heart and wake the soul
No longer begging on the dole
'Tis life, I say, and make it sure
Let's not move on 'til life is pure
I throw the arms out open wide
And shake the terror from the pride
Just throw away the dirty deeds
When last, it is I have been freed
To walk along the sandy shore
Quick! One look! We're back for more!

Whickwithy

So often, it is true
The reminisce you rue
Awakened from that long, lost sleep
That numbness that did slowly creep
Into my empty soul
The time has come, the fear is gone
No more to play the helpless pawn
For, now, I can be whole
Time no longer bears the brunt
Of broken dreams and listless front
In which to fire the coal
I walk on through the ferns and all
Awaiting the return of fall
Like lover who has long been lost
The other three are just the cost
So like an ache inside the bone
All unprepared, a sudden moan
I tolerate the other three
For in the past, I'm meant to be
For all the time from spring through frost
It's in the fall, my heart is tossed
Back to the beach, again, go I
The waves they smile but, also, fie
The worst of summer's come and gone
Too wet for me, this summer long
This time I grasp, though in the past
So softly held and, then, recast
To filter sadness through the sand
The sweetness left within the hand
The coolness of this ocean morning settles round the soul
It wakes to all those wondrous sighs and brings the heart near whole
I'm here to wander through this life, most ways, so all alone
A heart, it stirs, beneath the rain, at last a seed is sown
The haze it lifts, the glare is gone, I glimpse the soul divine
One day, one life, eternally, that heart and soul are mine
The mist it parts, at last I see, eternity I've won
For all of time and space, behold, the giant soul as one
The mysteries are hidden still, but answer's clear as light
Exultation now will come, I've shed the cloak of night

Just listen to the whisper as it tells of all to be
The numinous is certain and the notion sets us free
To read it once, must read it twice, a third time on its way
The answers there, between the lines, embedded in the play
No need for anger, fright, or hurt
There is no you and me
For life will just put on a spurt
To show that we are free
A pause in life, just now, is right to set the pace once more
The hammer rings, the thunder strikes, to shake the very core
The wonder of the shapeliness does dance to eyes that see
Vibration of the strings do stir for all eternity
All random sights and random thoughts do break upon the surf
For when, at last, I wander home they break upon my turf
The laughter ringing through the night, it is another song
The singing of the heartfelt joy can never do you wrong
A smile will brighten night and day, to mirror, if I may
When it is your on the way, I'll know it's time to play
Ah, this year of seasons, full, has been a troubled one
That wasn't in the plan at all, that's life beneath the sun
At last, once more, thank god it is, the coolness will return
For, at least, a little while no more the summer's burn
You'd say that I was two years old, sometimes, the way I think
As if the summer is now gone and autumn's on the brink
But, even though I know it's not, I like to think it's true
So, there it is, in many ways, I guess I am still two
It's something I am proud of, and that truly is the case
To keep the wonder, see the bitter gone without a trace
Like children's eyes I'll watch this life as long as I can see
For when the pain would linger on, somehow this sets me free
In living isolation is another way to race
But, then, you see, it's life and love that leave without a trace
I'll always live with open arms, though empty they may be
Those open arms are also part of that which sets me free
The ocean and the motion swell to something very fine
It's just about two weeks to go and, then, the beach is mine
All of those sandy folks are gone, once more, back to their home
A different beach it surely is, still, come low tide, I roam
And, as the seasons move through me, the tide sets pace through time

Whickwithy

Just like the beat within the verse brings life to heart and rhyme
For when the tide is low, then I dance and glide the coast
And when the tide is high, of all my work I, then, will boast
I mow the grass, I pull the weeds, I cut the wood, once more
But, when the tide is low, then, on the beach my heart will soar
A lot of verses written there, of that you can be sure
'Tis something found upon the beach that makes the soul feel pure
To just distill it down, complete, with bottle and a cap
It surely could be sold like that as cure for rat race trap
The castles made of sand are lost each day to tide and time
Do children learn a lesson there or is it just to prime
The children to the lesson learned that all things disappear
Along with summer sun, it's just another flame to sear
Or is it that the children clearly see it best of all
No meaning in the cheering and no reason for the pall
There's magic in the season's change and in the world at large
So many toss the heart a dream with entry free of charge
And on the border with the dream, like ocean to the coast
A deep expanse of hope and prayer will wash the soul foremost
But, even if the snow does fall upon the borderline
The tide will wash away the snow to clear this coast of mine
As open and serene as golden fields in summertime
'Tis where the heart is with a will and leaves the soul sublime
The coolness hit
It seems so fit
To start and end with fall
A time of heart, a time for pause
Reminiscent most of all
So much is hidden in the clause
A lifetime to recall
Just like the colors hide the flaws
Away, the worries all
The fall is saying, in its voice
It is your life, now live the choice
It's time to, now, "stand tall"
The beach is sketched as empty
With the people painted out
Of course, I am exemptly
Here for closing, final bout

Whickwithy

A little time is lent to me
There's much more I can spout!
Of course, the way I rattle on there'll not be time enough
The day the poem's year does end, they'll grab me by the scruff
Give another hundred years, I might just know my stuff
But, I will always plug away and sketch it out in rough
To sketch the seasons, there's a task, I hope that I've done well
The seasons are a beat of life and seem to cast a spell
Though poorly wrought it just might be, it is the tale I tell
To paint a picture of this life with seasons most of all
Emotions ran the gamut far along the seasons' wall
Elation, joy, with shock and fear, struck during last year's Fall
And scary, steadfast, wondrous time were there for Winter's call
The brightest, surging life in Spring but, then, there was the pall
The bitter gone, the sweet reigned Summer clouds above it all
Elation, heart, as always is, with autumn's windswept drawl
And, there I go, once more it is, I reminisce in fall
So many ways that fall is best
It follows after all the rest
The winter comes to cleanse the land
And springtime's rain gives life a hand
The summer's heat helps life expand
And, autumn celebrates so grand
Expanse of life now seen to end
To sum it all, it's here to lend
A little of the life we live
I learn to love and learn to give
The children back at school, once more, they romp outside my door
There is no doubt in this one's mind that, simply, they know more
It's nice to be reminded that this life holds joy and fun
Just take the time to see it all as seasons in the sun
And, now, the tale that wags the dog
Is seen through all but thickest fog
The swirls of mist are tossed, unseen
The dog and tail are lost between
The tale that needed telling, was, so I say, "what the heck"
Sometimes, I wandered on the way with mirrored introspect
It's quiet, now, the stores are shut throughout the tourist town
The echoes of the frenzy fade and local folks abound

Whickwithy

All softened, now, the notes and tune that play around the change
Those restless feelings come to fore, this life to rearrange
It seems so odd that it is new but, often, life is strange
The way in which the echoes will reflect the cool exchange
Transforming sand in little pools to deepest dells and marsh
And, then, back to the little pools just seems a little harsh
The flowers have all bloomed
All shades on through to white
Even though they're doomed
Their colors are still bright
The wood is stacked, the fireplace clean
No more the waiting in between
The morning birdsongs gone but, then,
It's sad to say, I know not when
I bundle up and contemplate
The coolness does invigorate
Preparing for the winter, see the squirrels run madly 'bout
I find I do the same on through this journey's final route
The time it ticks, the days pass by
Yet, still, the seagull's lonely cry
The wind picks up to sweep the soul
I face to winter's daunting role
So like the ocean's mass and size
The winter's role I now surmise
That boldly am I here and kept
So simply gone, at last windswept
Yes, flicker once across the screen
For just a glimpse that's sometimes seen
But of those perfect, windless days
With stillness born, the lion lays
It's viewed through sunlight's slanting rays
The words are lost, but heart does praise
The swirling thoughts of time and shore
What's often left, we seldom store
To pass on through the time, unknown
It's often plans are overthrown
The boon is farther than I thought
As time does pass away
But bowed and bent, you'll find me not

This heart does well portray
The changing life, days clear of rain
The wonder time, it comes again
This early, bright and wondrous fall
The tint on leaves just says it all
I'm marching down through endless time
I'll celebrate these loves of mine
The fickled days will come, I'm sure
To set the scale and bound the cure
But time, it ticks, as clock winds down
The seasons cycle, clock's rewound
We'll whirl away with colors strewn
The autumn's rainbow, fire and dune
Unlike the summer's prism pure
The red of kiss and sky's azure
The tossed emotions fired behind
Right through this heart and soul of mine
I'm pierced by feelings never worn
That never paused for pain or scorn
It is the will upon the way
So often, now, I sometimes say
I never hold the love at bay
The goal is seen, 'tween land and quay
The seeds all gone, all life is chance
We'll see in spring whose danced their dance
The sea breeze batters at the rocks
The fair wind travels round the stocks
Proud beauty in the woods stand tall
In summer, winter, spring, and fall
I ache to be that sturdy tree
There's strength in roots and leaves you see
Alone with fellows standing tall
Arrayed with strength among them all
But strength partakes a balanced view
The strength of all, not strength of few
And, in three seasons, shade it gives
To all the life that grows and lives
Beneath the arching canopies
That gently guards all that it sees

Whickwithy

The seasons, tides, and daylight change, of course, then, so do I
For all the changes in a year, a lifetime in a sigh
As north you go, the more the sunbeams change their willful way
The ebb and flow of tides reflects my moodiness per se
But, season come around, once more, to toll the bell of fate
It's pleasing just to listen close for words that tolerate
The glory of the sun is here, a boon so bright today
The story of a life in which the moon shall wash away
This yawning of a year
In which strange paces did abound
As through the stars we steer
And, on we go to life profound
The music of the spheres
Is just as real as is the sound
There's eternally a tear
Until all heart and life are found
For the song that you will hear
By which the soul is clearly bound
Is only for your ear
For which this music box is wound
But seasons, seasons flying by
A stroke of brush and paint
They wash the colors, then, let fly
Like blessings of a saint

So, sling the season's sparkle as it scatters 'cross the sky
And, fling the reason's nonsense up just like a newborn's cry
For, once again, it comes the time to dally round the dance
To raise the hand and bend the knee, no more the don'ts and can'ts
As if I stand upon a cliff with jagged rocks below
But, wings will spread and I will fly for in my heart I know
The seasons, gone, will come, again, from summer through to spring
Though the tide is rising, soon, the lowest tide will sing
Yes, we've wandered far this year from hearts to star and leaf
And walked the change and beach and woods, spent little time on grief
We've heard the waves and saw the surf and felt the heartstrings tug
No time is left to flicker on, just lead the way with hug
It feels as if we're parting ways so, deep within, I sigh
Our hearts have paced a little while but, now, I say, goodbye

Whickwithy

The time moves on and I do too
And, loving, deeply so, still true
I step, once more, to give a try
And hear the seagull's lonely cry
I offer up this whirlwind sigh
Enough to love, enough to try
For always will I stay the course
No loss of love and no remorse

October 1, 2009 Pine Point, Maine

Rhapsody

To have the joy of someone's life within one's own purview
No deeper honor to the heart within this life is due
A careful treatment is required, a heart that knows its way
Assured, the heart portrayed goes boldly forward, light and gay
To sing a song of understanding, hearts and love behold
To feel the life and live it right, fulfilling life as told
And, now, as it's time, I can change up the pace
To bring it all home and to know the realm's grace
Embracing the past, while I flourish in now
More life to be cast, heart beguiled, this I vow

The leaf and twig

The leaf holds softly to the twig it needs for life's support
The wind and rain and elements are part of its consort
Tentative connection held to that which gives it life
The poet warrior ponders this as wonder sings his fife
The leaf will pass and twig remain as seasons come and go
But, once again, the leaf returns, embracing season's flow
He sits, unmoving, through a time to ponder just a leaf
All of life moves past him, a peripheral motif
'Tis this necessity that drew him from his love and heart
To understand the universe in whole, not just in part
The leaf tied to the twig is as his life is tied to hers
Only in her presence, in her heart, his essence stirs

Infinity

Seldom a practiced exercise
Infinite focus with the eyes
No simulacrum compromise
No chance to focus on the lies
The latitude is emphasized
The purview must be recognized
The view is such as can't be matched
In depth and time, extent despatched
The soul can sense the great expanse
Unfettered by all circumstance
To change the focus in extent
From near to far, the dooms relent
To pass unto a wayward sea
Of life's dominions shrugging free

A study in beauty

Exposure to beauty repetitively
May cause some to ponder, inquisitively
And, others affected so primitively
Will balk at the beauty, demonstratively
While there are still others, definitively
Embracing enhances them creatively
And, sure there are some that disruptively
Reject the whole premise insensitively
But, rare are the ones that, superlatively
Embellish acknowledgement receptively

Pleasance

One thing in life that I would change
Shift mountain tops to rearrange
A way to ease your heart's distress
And, bring it all to coalesce
We will be one, but time's disdain
Has made this life as crowning vain
All agony I feel is for

The ache I left upon your door
I celebrate your life and mine
No thought could change that sweet to brine
But, only do I feel bereft
If lovely smile has nothing left
And, I have failed that single task
What question should the oarsmen ask
To steer a way along and through
To celebrate all thought of you
No sympathy is seeded
This life, as such, conceded
A steady stroke is needed
A choir of angels pleaded
To find the recompense
The steersman sets the course
No thought of life's remorse
A way is driven through
With thoughts of me and you
Preparedness commence
Like chopping wood for winter
Each log a single splinter
Of the fire within the soul
It will not end in fire
Or root the world's desire
To make of it a whole
The winter's chill will end with spring
And, to that end, my will does sing
Of warmth and cribs and eyes of Jewels
The glistening of melting pools
A sight that leaves the world unspent
And justifies all life's assent
That timing is of essence
We'll wander in that pleasance
When, once again, we meet

Solutions

A pulse is felt, it is enough, to navigate the day
A thrill runs through to fingertips assuring life's foray
But, underneath, a rumble builds, its ramping all through time
There's more to this than just the thrill, there's more to life and rhyme
The singing of the universe is aching to get through
A tone that runs along the thread, vibrating me and you
The winding road of life leads to the insight of the view
'Tis not the road but in the dance we find the answer to
The questions that can build a life to something more than pale
To make each moment thunder, with a life that's strong and hale
The path is sometimes hidden, brush and brambles clog the way
The tune becomes more difficult, the dancing seems to stray
Solutions for the moment will become a tightened noose
To break the chains, reclaim the life, and ease the dancing loose
Solutions for eternity necessitate the deed
Requiring one to hold the course, to heal instead of bleed
But, in the end, beginnings stir, the flower on the stem
Crowning life in something more, the hidden diadem
Now, the way is clearest and the path is smooth and straight
Just steady on, a patient heart, a will to now create
A view into eternity, essential to the task
The answer to the question mark before you ever ask
Seek the serendipity
A tempo set to destiny
Unending in its quality
All limits set by you and me
The rhythm's in the wind and in the air
The steps must sense with loving and with care
Subtly posed, accept the steps in kind
No knowledge helps except that life's divine

Symphonize

To track a cause unto its source, it must be run aground
To bring the thought unto the light, release the questing hound
The scent is caught, the trail is run, at last the source is found
Transcendent to the random thoughts, these thoughts, in essence, sound
In symphony with song of life, all notes and thoughts resound
Each step is gained, each measure writ, the instruments astound
No knowledge of the tune is known, the ways it quests abound
As notes all trip across the stage, the transients confound
Each step precedes the swing and dip, the dance of life is crowned
The stage is set, the flourishing of thoughts remain profound

Ethereal

A wisp of mist, a swirl of color, rising from the sea
Enchanter from some other realm; a gentle, sweet whimsy
A revel on the border of the wind and soft moiré
A pleasance passing in the night, all hesitance to slay
A crest of wave, a crescent beach, a splash of ocean spray
A sweetness felt within the air, a whimsical foray
A plume of pillows pressed beneath, so wondrous statuesque
The insubstantial lines that form a lovely arabesque
A chiming laugh that rings of bells and sings of sudden joy
A mix of sun and breath and cheer that makes a new alloy
A whisper that removes the chill, the spring that melts the snow
All composed within the song, the score of a maestro

A life worth living

Some endings are beginnings and some notes are not a score
Some lives are weary wanderings, an endless weary chore
But, presence and continuance are different things indeed
An end to all that's meaningless, a heart that's truly freed
Beyond the pale, in depths unknown, the will is found in need
To carry on and face the doom, the coin is now agreed
The whistle of the racing train seems slowly to recede

The whisper

Laid out upon the table are the rations of the day
A bit of sweetness, on the side, a sense of agapé
The trenchant and mercurial are set for slow sauté
A taste of bitterness intrudes upon the consommé
The windows open wide to bring the warmth of dawning ray
The scent of blooming life expands within the entryway
Standing there enshrouded by the light behind the door
The senses say, 'tis tale and wind of wand'ring troubadour
A mandolin in one hand and the other, metaphor
Behind the minstrel, trees and score
Out in the world, a brief rapport
A boulevard leads to the shore
Reflecting all the pains we wore
The wind in whistles speaks encore
The mandolin of evermore
The crashing waves of last uproar
The whisper says there's something more

Broken rhythms

The broken rhythms haunting me along my weary way
I tumble down a fractious frown, a lean and relic stray
Piano sitting idle and the bones of life denied
The measures written rhythmic are so broken in their stride
Distractions pile upon the heap, a feast of this and that
Poetic license brings a beat, the rhythm in a hat
The doom of life reminding me the ticking is for naught
Digging deep, within the heap, a rare inlay is sought
Surrounded by the rhythms as the smile begins to crest
The beat of life, once more, takes hold at harbinger's behest

More than willpower

Bad habits in the closet hid away
Not on the sleeve or podium, per se
The substance of long habits do reveal
They are not shaken by a will of steel
Surround them, understand them through the sounding
Each surface, crevice, crack is so resounding
A will that thrashes renders all the tracks
Those splintered thoughts are shattered by the axe
And still the habits wait within the wings
To pull at you, like hidden puppet strings
Undoing of a crooked life is slow
In increments so small, it seems not so
A sigh is born, the patience shows the scars
As constant as the twinkling of the stars
The heart, the heart brings will beyond what's known
It bring the note to clarity of tone
To sing the notes, to all extent unknown
Vibrations fill existence to the bone
The universe's murmur fills the soul
It settles in the heart to make it whole

Perfection

The fingertips reach out to touch all that the soul perceives
And, with the touch, the heart's reborn, in waiting, it receives
All answers to the questions asked, the many lifetimes spent
To find the answers, beat the drum, repay the gift that's lent
A wonder to the universe that cannot be replaced
Along the windings on the way, each life is surely traced
Some tales are told, some songs are sung of longing and remorse
But, with each step along the way, the story takes its course
Arrival in uncertain terms, the day will come at last
Retracing and replacing all the sorrows from the past

Intentions

Deep in whiteness, see me being torn
I come, at last, significance reborn
To tremble on the verge of distant realms
Surrounded by the weeping, silent elms
The typhoon tugs upon the tendrils tips
In all directions, now, the zephyr rips
The whisper's lost upon the swirling wind
All twists of fate upon the mast is pinned
A laugh is heard, it echoes on the rocks
Presaging the unwinding of the clocks
The tempest is unraveled on the beat
The windlass hauls the ravage indiscreet

That old familiar feeling

Time does tell a tale or two of bright and lucid dreams
Of whispers rising on the wind of shining, bright sunbeams
But, habits from a distant past arrive upon the scene
A ragged scalpel cuts across the vision in between
A feeling never spoken, just a sense from life before
Habits never broken, still conditioning decor
To break bad habit's wild embrace
All of life, one must retrace
Right back into the womb
Unspoken from the early years
Conditioned sense of silent tears
All life it will entomb
Destructive force, unwitting in its treason
Conditioning before one spoke with reason
The quirks that we all show upon the stage
Untrammeled by all thoughts of pain and rage
The answers lie in heaps among the past
Perception is the first attempt to cast
Transcending rote, the step that will surpass
And cancel frozen actions that amass
That old familiar feeling's often bane
It brings the haunt and, then, it brings the rain

Calm and joy

A presence felt, a known heartbeat
Sensing fullness, time complete
Anticipation, endless sigh
Eternity, it paints the sky
A thrill unmeasured pumps the blood
Surprise dreamtouch releases flood
The ripples form 'cross pools of rain
The sun bursts out from clouds of pain
Her heartbeats touch the soul, again
Fortune's child begins its reign
Penitence, that broken state
Borne in patience, consummate
The bourn is bright within purview
The mist has settled into dew
A pause has come, a final beat
Preceding symphony, complete

The focus

The wonders of this life would pull upon my mind
Distracting me from sweetness of your heady wine
But, now, the wonders I engage
Mysteries' footnote on a page
The focus and the rhyme is all so true
This deepest mystery in life is you

Prism dreams

I wonder, once again, what's fated
Prism dreams are reinstated
Cascade waves, once more, in time
Windswept words, once more, in rhyme
Weathered will now bears the brunt
The piercing stare that now is blunt
Turns inward to the farthest dreams
Naught of doom, though so it seems

Musings, metaphors, and mammocks

Life is like the clouds or stars or ripples on the ocean
But, grandest of them all, so like the universe in motion
The patterns seen depend upon the thoughts within ones mind
Superficial images, so often, what we find
Nothing seen, another view that is the way of some
And, then, of course, mechanicals will treat the view as numb
The whole that takes the breath away and leaves one in a state
Of richness served, much more than kings, the blessedness of fate
Answering the small and meek
Is the depth of view to seek
Complexity of clouds is smoothed by distance
And, to the breeze, they offer least resistance
Adapting form to breezes as they sway
Existing still, they bend their will away
The stars will spark but, far beyond, they light the cosmic tree
Twinkling through the black of night, arrayed for all to see
A scintillating spectacle that burns when one is near
Or, warms with gentle touch of heart through distances we steer
The ocean's ripples build to waves that span across the planet
Frothing far without release until it touches granite
The slightest ruffle in the water weaves with all the rest
Swirling in the tides of time to build the sweeping crest
The universe contains it all, the ripples, light, and storm
To pass beyond and coalesce the order and the form
Infinity's expanse defines, the goal as resolute
To reach for stars, to ride the clouds, and bathe in life's pursuit

Tumbleweed

The tumbleweed acquired the dust of countless, barren days
A disappointing life, it seemed, in oh, so many ways
The desert plain goes on and on, no end within one's sight
A struggle, once again, ensues, there is no end to plight
But, note, a disappointing life is in this case anointing
'Tis not to say, of this assured, that life is disappointing

Final edit

When the wind is past the trees
Upon the fields, it falls and flees
Free reign, at last, on past the wit
Upon its way with form and fit
The splendid days will come, at last
So wild and happy, firm and fast
To swing beyond the world's delight
Removing all that's false and trite
And, now, at last, the final edit
And, yet, I laugh, for who has read it

Ripples in the wind

The ripples in the wind we cannot see
And, yet, they fly across both land and sea
To tumble through the fabric of our lives
And from those ripples, all of life derives
A shift that's never witnessed in a breath
Seldom witnessed from a birth to death
How do we steer the craft to splendid cove
Through unseen ripples witlessly we rove
Attention paid to clouds and lightning strikes
Willy-nilly, plundered by the likes
The thunder adds more ripples to the wind
All progress towards our goal, we now rescind
A sense we must develop for the ripples
Or end our time as life's unwitting cripples

The doom

The warrior king sits brooding on his throne
His right hand grasps a goblet made of bone
He drinks the dregs of gloom from patient past
Empty now, the goblet crushed and cast
In his left, he ponders broken sword
And throws the blade, no longer realm's true ward

Passage

The shreds of sanity and tattered traits
Ripple in the wind through narrow straights
The passage through the narrow course confines
But stubborn intransigence well defines
The struggle 'gainst the obstacles erected
Refinements to the breaching well-perfected
The setbacks and the ticking of the clock
That leave the scars upon the weathered rock
The fingers lightly brushed across a scar
Breathes heart into the lifeless from afar

A poet's dream

As I attest, in awe, another time
Put pen to paper for another rhyme
To ponder, once again, that I'm attached
To beauty that I deem is so unmatched
A beauty even Time dares not to touch
As Time, a thrall, exalts in you as much...
But, here is where my pondering begins
Not only has Time spared, in you, his sins
But, revels so, enhances on each pass
So, as Time goes, your beauty gains in class
Beyond all wit that's known to memory
Unrivaled beauty grows for all to see
Breath-taking in its purity and style
I revel as time passes, all the while
The dream's to see that beauty, once again

Winter winds

Winter winds are having their last say
With anger as the elements betray
A warmth has come, no longer in its thrall
As life's respite is coming to us all
The shattered will of winter will now fall
The whisper with the strength of clarion call

The colors

A strength resides upon love's grace within eternal halls
No force of time or man can ever breach these sturdy walls
Upon the rampart's walk, impatience stirs, the passion calls
Across the land, the spell in winter's blight of guilt enthralls
But, slowly, now, enchanted land gives way to life and Spring
The crocus blooms, the squirrels romp, and birds begin to sing
The memories retain their force, the glistening returns
The sun upon the dew-filled land evaporates concerns
Despair and all its pitied ilk no longer hold them fast
Discoveries of life and love, the endless vistas vast
The land is well renewed as all the panic now subsides
Upon the mount of memories, the heart so boldly rides
From keep and through the gate, they canter through the broader world
To flowers thrown, and lances raised, the pennant is unfurled
Time has reinforced the colors of this endless love
The gifts are clear, the end is seen, the heart does rise above

The living throne

The words expressed that flutter by
Contend will all of life that I
am merely moving stone
They express a constant thought
Well-rivaled by a will that's wrought
Upon a living throne
Unremarked upon the wind
Undisturbed and underpinned
That will knows more than I
Echoes of some meaning measure
Rise above what vain does treasure
And, so, the flutters die

Self-limiting

Where the limits of this place in which we spend our time
Encumbered by the concrete and the endless paradigm
What limits, that restraint of bonds, when chains of life unlock
How many of the dungeons walls are fictions of the clock
A ray is cast upon the floor from crack within the wall
A color felt, a rhythm seen, sets free enchanting call
Transformation, once again, removes the mortar's hold
To crumble all the shattered walls as sanities unfold
The resolutions that we reach are tales of wit and wag
Intuition leads to life beyond the broken crag
Look back upon the crumbled walls, surprise at what is wrought
A pile of dust, insights unique, and tales of lessons taught

Tremours

What is it that we seek in what we say
What tremours through expanse of walking clay
Will drive a thought to something more than dross
So that, no longer, view life as a loss
But, hidden luster in the very core
Of everything we touch and, something more
The tremours build, the wisdom shakes
And, as the notion reawakes
The age-old patterns fall upon the floor
Like so much rubble swept on out the door
Shed all the doubt and clutter from the din
As life takes hold, supply a suiting grin
The tremours settle and we pause, once more
To find that luster hidden in the core

Eternal Towers

The title courtesy of Ralph Waldo Emerson.
Variations on a theme.

Far off, in distance, do I see
Eternal Towers watching me
The rubble standing in between
As blind as night, before not seen
So on, upon the threshold bare
I stumble through will little care
The dawn seeps up beyond the towers
The fear departs, the canon cowers
For, now, the light is opening
A way in which the wind will bring
The scent of troubles to be manned
The rough and shoddy to be banned
Revealing all to sight now clear
The troubles that I held so dear
They crumble, insubstantial dust
Enthralled no longer by the must
Of broken will to disappoint
The towers, now, the lights anoint
The future rolls into a point

Dangling participle

The poor little dear, left all alone, and at the end, to wag
The participle, once again, has something that will lag
It finds itself the center of attention for a span
For who is it that leaves alone what participles can
Singing, humming, smiling, as displayed without the frocks
It twirls, for all, and takes a bow, for ways in which it knocks

Strength of Habit

Conditioned from the time of birth
Or cued from things of little worth
The habits that we all entail
And lost beyond a false dark trail
The darkness of our legacy
Brings such a plague that we could be
Ensnared upon the endless tread
To live a life that's truly dead
To break the bonds of habits' dread
At last, to deem the soul as fed
Unencumbered by the waste
At last, the physical to taste
Break open to a newborn state
To lives and loves that truly rate
This precious moment set unto
The ring of bells that sing the due
Human to the nth degree
And all it takes is that we see
Ladies first

The martinet

The martinet stands sturdy with a pensive visage worn
Ramrod straight, no slack allowed, and to the strictness sworn
The poor, old martinet has not a clue about the sward
Manner, mores, and values are just etchings on a board
Attempts to be mistaken as a person with some sense
Mistakes are made, so come the rules and, never, he relents
Was taught it's worst to look a fool, but mirror never shows
The fact that martinet is fool in rigidness he chose

Roots

My roots so deep into this earth
Bring strength and vision for rebirth
Each and every day, this change
To watch the picture rearrange
To see all life, before my eyes
Bursting change mid harkened cries
To picture life in all forays
From solemn to ecstatic craze
To stand above the ocean's wave
And watch the ripples foam and rave
Intuit sense through time and space
To which of spectrum's ends we race
Balanced on the quantum's edge
Will last until we, flound'ring, fledge
So many notions shed upon the way
Like winter clothes are shed for brighter day
New notions come to try their chance to play
Some good, some bad, some hinting at the fey
This four dimensioned image that I've drawn
Will we hold, denying feint or fawn
Speculation in the wings of where the cultures flow
Swirling mists sometimes do part but, seldom, do they show
The thoughts conceived
The web that's weaved
But, on and on, we go

The Scene

The scene that I look out upon has never slightly changed
And, yet, somehow, and, often, it is all so rearranged
As if a thread were pulled and all the fabric were let loose
And, then, a magic hand would thread it back for my reuse
Or, like kaleidoscope that jumbles all within its view
A shattering of broken glass that slowly does ensue
Becoming more, each day, each year, as time does slowly pass
That brightens through the window's view, a well-defined stained glass

Strings

Preconceived, the notions, that we carry 'neath our brow
And, carry with us, all our lives and, always, to them, bow
From a past, so deeply gone, and from today's barrage
Roll up the door, toss open wide, see clutter in garage
Remarkable or nonsense, still, it all just seems the same
Recordings, playing, in our heads, the source unknown to blame
We wander life, as in a maze, so blind and, often, lame
Seeking for some glory or some thoughts of fling or fame
We often hunger, aimlessly, no meal, an empty plate
The strings of notions, pre-conceived, keep pulling at our fate
The marionette's distracted from all thought of life and grace
Confusion reins, as swells the pains, you've joined the human race
The hidden puppeteers are nimble as we swing and dance
So seldom do we look askew, no mirror for our glance
Those thoughts of fame now all but gone
As time goes ticking slowly on
The strings becoming frayed
And, now, the game is played
Unto its very end

Fragments

The fragments of a passion fill the air
From senses that have longed to fill with care
Melodious, in concert with what's played
The fragrance spreads beyond the time arrayed
All living things are vibrant from the touch
That ripples through to make of life so much
The coruscating colors so alive
As passions for this life, once more, survive

Channels of the heart

A loving heart, she owns in full
Like tides, its unrelenting pull
My love that lights the air
Beyond all loving ever known
Rings so deep the wondrous tone
Of life and heart and care
Like magic that can light a life
A charm that makes each moment rife
With revel sans compare
It may be bridled in this life, small chance to fill the pond
But still, she holds within her grasp the magic of the wand
And, I have been so blessed to have felt the loving touch
Of she, who loves, unending, casting spell that means so much
Unto this day, the spell on heart has kept me breathing air
A student ruminating on all life and heart and care
The tiny wisp of guidance through the smallest open frame
Has built a fortress sturdy through which only loving came
Though long I've ached for more the touch
A time is spent on learning such
That I may own the dream
Of loving her with heart nonesuch
Preserve through time what means so much
Eternity, I deem
But, time ticks on, commitments must be met
Within this life, the spider wove the net
To trap two hearts at distances apart
But, hidden rivers channel through the heart

The Cleansing Rain

The lightning strikes, the thunder shakes, across the sky's expanse
And rattles deeply through the lives, in sharp and thrumming cants
The story's new perspective viewed is in the light, revealed
All distant, foreign, aching thought is, in the end, repealed
In the distance, far off, seen
There comes the rain to wash it clean
And, when the clouds have cleared and, finally, part
All that's left is loving in the heart

Whickwithy

The reason for unreason

in the depths of distant time a sentience emerged
Onward, upward, was the passion that their essence urged
But, chaos did ensue for they had made a slight mistake
Embarrassed and unwitting, they had thrown at heart a stake
Love and honour were the ones that fell upon the ground
And, witness to the sad affair, all reason was unsound
A pall occurred when mention of the act was ever made
So silence and unreason took the stage and farce was played
To see the truth and shout it, only echoes do return
Until the truth is evident, for all, the heart will burn
Rage and fury settle in, for price that we have paid
A challenge made, a gauntlet thrown, that reason will cascade
I cannot seem to raise the tide, a glamour does reside
Will is not enough, it seems, to raise the ocean wide
But, will and effort integrate, an iron without match
A hammer built for all mankind to break unreason's latch
Forged in our humanity, while flames were flying high
A breath of life for all of us, a message in a sigh
Life and living's hard enough without unreason's weight
Take the chance of life and heart and, then, you will relate
There is an answer to the drum that's heard on summit's peak
A celebration of this life, undo the havoc's wreak

Moments and lifetimes

A moment long forgotten and a lifetime that's renewed
Upon a lonely mountain when that moment was eschewed
The heart alone can tell the tale that lifts us to the peak
Traversing all these moments to find life in what we seek
A moment's thought is spent upon all that which has been lost
The weariness that wanes the heart as moments will accost
Rippled deck for chosen cards, just fling them from the stack
A life that's full of living mid the moment's heart attack

Rhythm of the eye

Repair, at last, the rhythm of the eye
Make sense of all of this of which I spy
The pans are known
The rhythm shone
And, with each beat
I feel the heat
And miss the wholesome sigh
The dissonance perceived is something less
The action and the nonsense needs redress
The wit is thin
The nail is pin
The greed is known
Airs overblown
Beyond the pale I wait in eagerness

Naïveté

A simple thought, not glamour bound, belief in all one sees
Such frankness at the charge of life, no thought of angst that flees
A mantra through the depths of time, "I will naïveté"
A view to match the tides of life, a will that will be free
No shackles bind, no fetters trail, the arms are open wide
To take in all the breadth of life, the wonder that I ride
Encouraging the canter as the wind is felt so cool
The pace is set, horizons roll, the heart becomes the fuel

The leaf

A single leaf upon the water flowing down the stream
Ripples in the water push the leaf along a scheme
A stick may drag, a rock may swirl, the leaf's path undefined
But, still the leaf goes on its way accepting course assigned
To tumble down the falls of chance to rumble in the tide
The swirling, frothing, mists enshroud, a moment to abide
But, out it goes, still moving on, relentless is the ride
Upon the times that fortune grants, with grace the tree supplied

Alone

Alone and lonely are two different things
'Tis satisfaction with oneself that brings
Accrual of the sense of life's true test
By pondering the heart of living's quest
To mount the wave through ocean's surging tide
Unaware of modesty or pride
To balance on the sharpest razor's edge
To wash away the gritty sands that dredge
Through all the waste of time's acknowledged aide
To reason like the waterfall's cascade
Tumbling to the vastness of the sea
At last, alone, finality's decree

Lightning

Hand that floated to the side, the flicker of the wrist
Lightning flies from fingertips as fingers roll from fist
Laid low all wasted efforts, resurrecting will and way
Eternity a moment in the scope of agape´
Deep within the boundaries of all that life presents
The impetus unlimited, the heart and soul assents
To bring about a world that is unfettered by the fears
A world that's unrestrained by needless shedding of the tears

Moon Shadows

The silence smothers all of mankind's sound
The moon's bright shadows sharply cast aground
Just a whisper coming from the trees
A rustle in the shadow that agrees
Enchantment rules the sliver and the moon
The whispers and the rustlings do commune
Does light or shadow tell the mythic tale
Of lunar wizardry in light so pale
The larkings in the shadows now resume
The shadows are the bride, the light the groom
Something reflects shadows into light
Suddenly from shadow comes the knight

Existence

The beauty of existence as reflected in a leaf
The beauty that results in coming of steadfast belief
That beauty is as beauty does but so much more than that
That beauty as the central theme brings lustre to the matte
To find the beauty hidden in a face without a smile
Discovering true beauty in the heart and not the style
Discerning depths of meaning and the reason for the ride
Delving deep into the panorama to decide
That life is not an witless task of levers to be plied
Nor pained experience in which it is one must abide
Wake up and see the image in reflecting window pane
So soon the storm and darkened clouds at last begin to wane
And leaf, belief and honoring of beauty will remain

Feyderith

I wandered down a wilding course
And, left behind, with no remorse
The paltry and the pine
I took the path with unsure heart
The shattered window took apart
The wisdom to define
At last, the quest did take a turn
With blazing light, the world did burn
Away the clouds of mind
A picture painted with the hand
Brings color to the place I stand
Along with life refined
Like springtime coursing through the veins
The pulse of life and love remains
To bolster all inclined
To wash away the sudden doubt
And leave the crippling pale without
A way in which to bind
To Feyderith the course is set
To Kings and Knights and Dames well met
At last, the way is mine

The whisper in the trees

You hear it now? the sound is deep
It tells of soft, unending sleep
The silence built on sound
The vastness all around
The spright is seen
The bright between
The leaves breathe in and out
The pale light wanders on a seam
The mist drifts in along a beam
The rustle of the doubt
To break the spell
No one can tell
The whisper is devout

Unscripted

All the wonders of this life I ponder
Through vast array of miracles I wander
What in this world, alone, makes life complete
The longing duly filled, abyss replete
A hint is found within your subtle grace
The corner of the eye perceives a trace
A glinting of the spark that sets the pace
A sense that, here at last, with heart and lace
'Tis not the cupboard 'neath the stairway's steps
Long forgotten cobwebs, brief concepts
That rattle through the mind upon the way
Through scattered miracles in vast array
Protecting heart's thin walls in time's of need
Seeing way through false and crippled creed
But, steady as the gaze upon your eye
The sense of hope remains, again, I try
The answer is this heart of you and I

In Feyderith

The wind it sways and all life swings within the bounds of time
The land arrayed from plains to sweep through mountains as they climb
With life so full, upon this land, no measure can they name
Oh, Feyderith, the land of light, embraced by all who came
Your rivers, they ripple with gentlest touch
The ocean enfolds, as if so to clutch
The fields of dawn swaying away to and fro
The foothills will answer with morning sun's aglow
Bright Feyderith, you live
The people built of sturdy stone a Castle and a Keep
Though villages of friendly folk is where they always sleep
A benefice so burgeoning with all that people need
The very land itself allows no withering or weed
There is no king upon the blessed land
For all of man will lend a willing hand
Surrounded by the mountains tall
No ill wind can there ever fall
Sweet Feyderith, you give
'Tis best to survey far and wide, upon the stone plateau
The breath it takes, a sense of yore, a feeling that you know
There is no better life than this
The land gives love and gentle kiss
To Feyderith, I'm true
When the day of last has come unto so weary bones
When last of breath expelled with all the life this body owns
My fealty still, with pledge so bound
Throughout the land my voice will sound
Dear Feyderith, renew

Storms

As the storm approaches land the silence starkly looms
Darkness overcomes the day like empty, paneless rooms
The wind picks up, the waves rush on, the shore becomes a foam
The sense is of the wolves that run, along the crest they roam
The thunder rocks the cliffs of life, the lightning shatters dreams
The past seems but a memory, the lost horizon gleams
The storm will pass as all storms do
A moment's lapse, no need to rue
The rain comes pouring down

Renewal

Whirling of the wind makes such a case
Stirrings in the heart we can't replace
Sense of time expands to fill the plea
Wash of waves which also holds the key
Seasons in the north swing life around
Surf upon the sand brings home the sound
Sweetness hidden in the honeycomb
Notes that sing in time to metronome
Tree consents to summons of the leaf
Rustling waters through the living reef
Maybe, most of all, the flower's glee
That bring to life the color's bold decree
Energy escorts the coming spring
A universe runs through the blood to sing

Allegory

As if so sculpted by the crescent of the silver moon
And brushed, in depths and colors, with the rainbows of high noon
The glistening reflections of the tide will spray the scene
Awashed with waves of tidal strength that sprinkle in between
A picture so is born within the sweep of all that's been
The brushstroke's fine detail reveals the subject's kith and ken

Knight defined

The knight is one who holds the life of everyone to heart
Who bows to all and asks of none to take a paltry part
His life is given to the land and to the people there
He gives to all his gentleness, his loving, and his care
Most people in sweet Feyderith have learned the manner true
So Knights and Ladies fill the land and paradigms they hew
Tossed apart like waves off cliff, when foolish make their claim
That life is just obsession that the strongest boldly aim
To grovel for a sliver's not the reason why we came
In Feyderith, this lesson has been learned beyond intent
That life is for the living and each gesture truly meant
Integrity and dignity when facing foul or fair
With patience and the song of life, the lion in his lair
Honor-bound and willing to bring joy to those with none
The knight who holds the thunder in his gauntlet's grasp has won

The Murder of Crows

The murder of crows had awaited the breath, that first glowing, bright crescent of dawn
From trees up above, they surveyed all the grounds, from the river to castle to lawn
They spoke of their tales of the winds and the wings, of the feathers, the beak, and the claw
Soaring above, they saw all of life, yet so little they measured with awe
The carriage they saw as it swept through the day, on its path to the castle it seemed
Another such folly they spied every day and a waste of their time so they deemed
No curious call came from beaks in the trees, not the least little thought nor disdain
It paused on its way as the door opened wide and a creature debarked on the plain
As the murder did see what it was that so graced on the steps to the grass from the hatch
A flutter of feathers disturbed all the crows and spoke boldly of beauty unmatched

Whickwithy

Passion and beauty

I ponder the span, the progression through time
The wonder of life that's contagioned with rhyme
The passion and beauty of life is the scent
For which I will live, as this coil is unbent
It is what the revel is always about
The fragrance of breeze is no longer in doubt
The pillars of life that brace the sane mind
The passion and beauty, the grace and the kind
It fills all the air as I wander the ways
Of glorious times and most glorious days
Built upon passion and graced with the presence
Of beauty around me, in form and in essence
To paint with the colors of beauty and passion
A life can be measured in just such a fashion
A spell to avoid all the fears of a tragic last call
Passion and beauty, the keys to the magic of all

Banners

Array the night with wisp and whim
The stars are bright and colors dim
And, in the east, a hint of light
Banners fly from wan to bright
The wind picks up to tell the tales
Of joy untold, of light unveiled
The sidhe fly their banner raised
All pomp and circumstance unfazed
The lawn that sprawls across the vale
The brawny summits gird and scale
At last, the welcome horn is sung
Withal, the churches bells are rung
The revels, far and wide, unpin
Excitements of the day begin
The place transformed from staid to wild
All, by brightness, now beguiled
All hearts are warm, as are the smiles
All confidence to brave the wiles
Rejoice!

Index

A broken way	77	Crystal clear	41
A cozy little life	45	Dangling participle	126
A fairy tale	5	Daunting Realms	14
A life worth living	116	Deep in thought	16
A poet's dream	123	Delusions of grandeur	78
A study in beauty	113	Despair	73
A way forward	78	Destiny	58
All heart	65	Devastation	52
Allegory	137	Do you understand?	69
Alone	133	Dragon's paw	15
Await the day	32	Dream vision	6
Balance	50	Dreamland	22
Banners	139	Dreamscape	21
Best of both worlds	71	Elopement	73
Beyond the wind	75	Endings	27
Bifrons	4	Eternal Towers	126
Birds	66	Ethereal	116
Blossoms	70	Everlast	34
Brightness	49	Existence	134
Broken rhythms	117	Fantasies and Joy	70
Calm and joy	120	Feyderith	134
Caverns of the mind	2	Final edit	122
Channels of the heart	130	Footsteps in the snow	67
Chocolate truffe	66	Foreign lands	20
Confidence and doubt	72	Fractals	52
Crippled tongue	52	Fragments	129

Freedom	68	*More realms of the mind*	6
Friends	50	*More than willpower*	118
Gaia	42	*moss and bark*	23
Golden sounds	65	*Musings, metaphors, and mammocks*	121
Grand	29		
Guidance	33	*Naïveté*	132
Guidance, second version	37	*No Name*	56
Head up	28	*Now until end of winter*	24
Images of last resort	34	*Of kings and castles*	3
imagineers	32	*Open Wide*	40
Immediatement	39	*Open Wide*	76
In Feyderith	136	*Passage*	123
Incarnations	28	*Passersby*	33
Index	140	*Passion and beauty*	139
Infinity	113	*Passion's play*	4
Innocence	63	*Past Participle*	11
Intentions	119	*Patience*	57
Juggernaut	28	*Perfection*	118
Kingdom	20	*Petals*	61
Knight defined	138	*Petals 2*	73
Lagniappe	8	*Picturesque*	59
Landscaping	54	*Play to the passion*	74
Life's cornucopia	63	*Pleasance*	113
Light and shadow	55	*Poems*	25
Lightning	46	*Poetry*	12
Lightning	133	*Poetry*	79
Mirrors	16	*Poetry too*	10
Mirrors, again	74	*Prism dreams*	120
Moire'	26	*Realms of amazement*	29
Moments and lifetimes	131	*Realms of the mind*	5
Moon Shadows	133	*Reflections*	24

Renewal	137	Synergist	32
Resolve	11	That old familiar feeling	119
Rhapsody	112	The bard	69
Rhythm of the eye	132	The challenge	47
Rhythms of Life	27	The Cleansing Rain	130
Ricochets of the heart	83	The colors	124
Ripples	72	The concrete and the wind	66
Ripples in the wind	122	The crime	9
Ripples in time	39	The crowded sea	39
Ripples on the wind	25	The Dark	49
Ripples too	55	The depths	37
Room full of mirrors	18	The doom	122
Roots	128	The drum	35
Seasons	84	The End	64
Self-limiting	125	The final say	19
Serendipity's plan	80	The fire in the mind	20
Shadows	54	The first day of your life	58
Shatterfall	17	The focus	120
Shining bright	65	The forest and the trees	71
Silences	41	The Forest floor	22
Silly boy	67	The Fury	54
Small breakthroughs	1	The gloom	10
Smoking embers	18	The growing day	62
Solutions	115	The heart of fire	59
Springtime	65	The hounds of life	2
Stirrings	71	The Impossible Day	61
Storms	137	The Iron Will	69
Strength of Habit	127	The joy of life	40
Strings	129	The Last Bastion	68
Sway	40	The leaf	132
Symphonize	116	The leaf and twig	112

The life and times	38		The will of the wind 2	26
The living throne	124		The wind	68
The martinet	127		The wonder	19
The Murder of Crows	138		Think again	69
The mystery of the Tapestry	47		Thoughts	31
The ocean's waves	67		Three travelers	82
The perfect storm	29		Threnody	50
The program	45		Threshold	23
The puzzle	16		Tossed Salad	15
The Rainbow Knight	1		Transform	13
The reason for unreason	131		Transformation	30
The Rhyme	13		Tremours	125
The Scene	128		Trusting life	41
The sea	76		Tumbleweed	121
The sea of life	46		Unreserved love	52
The shore	53		Unscripted	135
The titan struggle	60		Warrior king	14
The Traveler	81		Waves	72
The Traveler's tale	3		Waves too	51
The Travelers	80		Where away?	57
The Treehouse	30		whippoorwill	67
The universe and all	75		Winter nights	51
The wandering ways	77		Winter winds	123
The way forward	79		Wonderfall	27
The weaver and the wizard	7		Worlds apart	7
The whisper	117			
The whisper in the trees	135			
The wilderland	56			
The will of the wind	25			

www.ingramcontent.com/pod-product-compliance
Lightning Source LLC
Chambersburg PA
CBHW051943160426
43198CB00013B/2284